UNIT

731

TESTIMONY

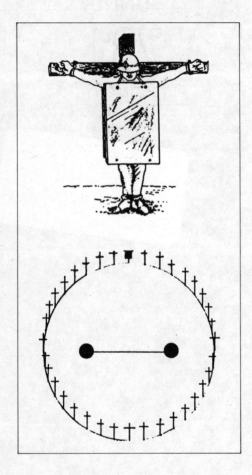

UNIT

731

TESTIMONY

Hal Gold

(Frontispiece) This diagram gives a general overview of the experiments conducted at the Anda testing field.

YENBOOKS
2-6, Suido 1-chome, Bunkyo-ku, Tokyo 112, Japan

© 1996 by YENBOOKS

LCC Card No. 95-60907
ISBN 4-900737-39-9

First edition, 1996

Printed in Japan

Table of Contents

Acknowledgments   8

Foreword   9

Part 1: Historical Overview

1. Background of Japanese Biological Warfare   17
   A Proud Medical Tradition   17
   Ishii Shiro   23
   Manchuria   26
   The Stage Is Set   29

2. A New Type of Warfare   32
   The Fortress/Bacteria Factory   32
   End of the Fortress   36
   Pingfang   38
   Satellite Facilities   48
   Ties to the Civilian Sector   59
   Ishii's Battlefield Debut   62

3. Creating Pathology   67
   Rodents and Insects   67
   Four Areas of Experimentation   70

4. End and Aftermath   86
   Attempted Biological Warfare Against
      the Americans   86
   Covering the Traces   92
   American Occupation   94
   Superpower Jockeying   101

5. Unit 731 in Modern Times   116
   The Teikoku Bank Incident   117
   Japanese Biological Warfare Data in
      the Korean War   123
   Shinjuku Shock   126
   The Unit Leaders in Peacetime   139
   Postwar Careers: Plum Positions   141

Part 2: Testimonies

Introduction   147
Researcher attached to Unit 1644 (Anonymous)   150
Virologist attached to Unit 731 (Anonymous)   152
Lecture, "Unit 731 and Comfort Women"
   (Nishino Rumiko)   159
Youth Corps member (Anonymous)   166
Hygiene specialist (Wano Takeo)   175
Hygiene specialist (Anonymous)   178

Kenpeitai member (Iwasaki Ken'ichi)   188

Three Youth Corps members (Anonymous)   189

Nurse attached to Unit 731 (Akama Masako)   198

Kenpeitai officer (Naganuma Setsuji)   200

Army doctor (Yuasa Ken)   204

Civilian employee of Unit 731 in Tokyo
(Ishibashi Naokata)   214

Youth Corps member attached to Unit 731
(Ogasawara Akira)   219

Professor emeritus at Osaka University
(Nakagawa Yonezo)   221

Member of the Hygiene Corps
(Tomioka Heihachiro)   222

Soldier stationed at Pingfang (Shinohara Tsuruo)   227

Soldier attached to Unit 731 (Ohara Takeyoshi)   234

Nurse attached to Unit 731 (Sakumoto Shizui)   235

Intelligence officer (Ogura Yoshikuma)   236

Army major and pharmacist attached to Unit 731
(Anonymous)   239

Army major and technician attached to Unit 516
(Anonymous)   241

Ishii Shiro's driver (Koshi Sadao)   241

Pharmacist attached to the laboratory at Dalian
(Meguro Masahiko)   243

Captain, Japanese Imperial Army (Kojima Takeo)   244

Select Bibliography   251

PHOTOGRAPHS *on pages* 128–136

Acknowledgments

Several people deserve to be mentioned here for the invaluable aid which they rendered in the creation of this book. Testimonies came to the author in the form of faxes or photocopies through the generous cooperation of the Secretariat of the Central Organizing Committee for the Unit 731 Exhibitions in Tokyo. Professor Eda Kenji and Professor Eda Izumi of Kyoto also assisted me in accumulating these materials. Ota Masakatsu of Kyodo News Service provided valuable information also.

Finally, I wish to extend my sincerest thanks to my editor, David Friedman, whose finely tuned editorial eye, disdain for rest, and familiarity with Japanese language and history were invaluable in turning my manuscript into a book.

Foreword

Some four decades following the end of World War II, details concerning the Imperial Japanese Army's Unit 731, which researched and conducted biological warfare, began surfacing with startling impact. Information about this outfit, at whose hands an estimated three thousand Manchurians, Chinese, Russians, Koreans, Europeans, and Americans were killed, had remained largely hidden over the years, either by governmental control or a code of silence adhered to by its former members themselves. Then, newly revealed information stirred interest in an era which Japanese officialdom has been trying to wash away with the detergent of neglect. Japan has been told to leave the past behind and move ahead told to new ties of friendship and commerce with other countries. Yet while business ties develop, and amity is proclaimed to be spreading, old facts emerging as recent revelations increase their magnetic attraction and pull us into a reexamination of what happened then—and again incite us into debates of how and why.

It can be argued that probably no school system anywhere teaches true history; only the degree of rear-

rangment varies. For the years during which the research units were active, the chasm between history
and Japan's official stance yawns wide. For years, Unit
731 "did not exist." Requests and demands not just
for monetary compensation but for mere recognition
of history and apology have been brushed away, turned
down because "compensation has been made at government levels." Instead, Japan offers its dedication to
"world peace" with statements that are as vague as
they are eloquent.

Information on Japan's consumption of live human
beings as biological test material has been surfacing
for many years now. As with the comfort women issue,
however, there has never been a jolt of sufficient volt-
age to rock the national government into acts of con-
trition or compensation. Rather, it has been local
governments who have opened their eyes to history.
The efforts of local governments, in conjunction with
high degrees of volunteer activity in their areas, can be
credited with bringing the Unit 731 Exhibition before
the eyes of Japanese in sixty-one locations over the
course of a year and a half. The exhibition, in whose
final days this book was begun, was arranged by a
central organizing committee in Tokyo, and each locality which wanted to plan a local exhibition had to
raise its own funds and find its own venue. There was,
of course, an admission fee to enter the exhibit, and so
for the visitors it could be considered a self-financed
course in the history omitted by orthodox education.

The shock to the Japanese people was predictable.
In spite of the occasional documentary coverage or
newspaper article, Unit 731 was largely unknown and
unthought of. It sat safely outside the scope of the
consciousness of most Japanese. True, some attention

was drawn to Unit 731 when the Japanese government was taken to court for not permitting factual accounts of it in school textbooks, but even those with some knowledge of the Ishii organization had their eyes opened at the exhibits.

Several factors have conspired to keep Unit 731's activities from receiving the attention they so richly deserve. The decades of concealment of the outfit's history were partly the fruit of the Japanese central government's reputed skill at inactivity, along with its priority on avoiding all manners of controversy, whether domestic or international. Evidence also failed to surface simply because there were no survivors among the victims of Unit 731; all were eliminated before the end of the war. Then, there was the combination order-threat by commanding general Ishii Shiro himself that former unit members were to "take the secret to the grave." Obedience to the command was probably not at all difficult for those surviving Japanese members of the unit who could have borne witness but would have felt scalpels turned in their own hearts were their children to ask, "Daddy! How could you do something like that?"—and feel it even more acutely in their later years when the question would be prefaced with "Grandpa."

This last fact highlights an even more astonishing result of the exhibition. Surviving members of Unit 731 who had sworn to remain silent about their memories came out before the public to testify—to confess—and finally unburden their minds. After a half century of silence, they told. Some could tell all but their names, and retained that one secret before the public: an omission meaningful to them, but a minor exclusion for those of us more interested in their stories than in their identities. Others identified themselves openly. Some reached the point of weeping with equal openness, as they looked back through decades of silence to stir up ugly recollections.

But those who are coming forward now, after some half-century of silence, are among the most forceful in pressing for the story to be told. Additionally, a limited number of members of the post-war generation—scientists, doctors, writers—are searching out the survivors, doing their own research, and informing the public through writings and lectures. Outrage and shame span the generations. Exhibition sites generally have a desk where visitors may write their impressions and comments. Attendees from elementary school on up have recorded the shock of the history lesson.

There are several reasons why the code of silence has evaporated at this late hour. Whatever these motivations might be, however, we can be grateful that the grave did not get all the truth. One focus of this book will be the actual words of those who helped conduct Japan's biological warfare human experimentation program.

The exhibition itself, the reactions it provoked, and the testimonies of former unit members who came forth and spoke out were all driving factors behind the creation of this book. It is as important for these events to be available to English-readers as it is that Japanese know them. Some of the testimonies and statements presented here were originally given at lecture programs which the author attended, recorded, and translated. At other programs in different parts of the country, testimonies were obtained with the cooperation of the local organizing committees. An independent team sought out former Unit 731 members and produced a video series which was another source. A few of the testimonies were told to other people who then reported on them at lectures or in print.

The recent declassification under the Freedom of Information Act of some documents that had been sealed for years also played an important role in the creation of this book. Events in the former Soviet Union likewise brought about a freeing of material formerly kept hidden away. Some Japanese documents have also been declassified, making them available to researchers. In the end, however, the most thought-provoking source of public information on Japan's human experiments comes from those who were there, then emerged from silence and provided the personal accounts which lead us back to the crimes with distressing credibility. These firsthand recollections make mockery of statements which attempt to smooth down the edges of the cruelty and racism that made Unit 731 possible.

PART

1

HISTORICAL OVERVIEW

1
Background of Japanese Biological Warfare

A Proud Medical Tradition

In all wars up until the Russo-Japanese War, it had been known that the "silent enemy"—disease—took a greater toll of lives among fighting men than did bullets. With the outbreak of the conflict with Russia, Japan made history by resolving to learn from her mistakes. Chastened by the waste represented by sickness-induced casualties that she had suffered in her recent war with China, she paid an extraordinary amount of attention to curbing battlefield illness. By the beginning of the twentieth century, her scientists were already gaining fame for their work, and feathers in their caps included discovery of the causes of beri-beri and dysentery. One strain of bacteria, the Shiga bacillus, even carries the name of its Japanese discoverer, Dr. Shiga Kiyoshi. The Western press termed the Japanese "scientific fanatics," a telling commentary on the lack of scientific awareness in other countries of the world, especially in military medicine. By contrast, Japan's army had come to be a—if not the—world leader in this field.

A perspective on Japanese military medicine at the time of Japan's war with Russia in 1904–05 is offered by a U.S. Army doctor, Louis Livingston Seaman. The Japanese granted him the privileges of a foreign military attaché, and he accompanied Japanese troops in Manchuria during the Russo-Japanese War. In addition to visiting field and base hospitals in Manchuria, he also observed hospitals in Japan. After the war, he published a book titled *The Real Triumph of Japan: the Conquest of the Silent Foe.* In it, he writes that

> the history of warfare for centuries has proven that in prolonged campaigns the first, or open enemy, kills twenty per cent of the total mortality in the conflict, whilst the second, or silent enemy, kills eighty . . . This dreadful and unnecessary sacrifice of life, especially among the Anglo-Saxon races, is the most ghastly proposition of modern war, and the Japanese have gone a long way toward conquering or eliminating it . . .
>
> I unhesitatingly assert that the greatest conquests of Japan have been in the humanities of war, in the stopping of the needless sacrifice of life through preventable disease . . .
>
> In our war with Mexico, the proportion of losses was about three from disease to one from bullets, and in our great Civil War nearly the same proportion obtained . . . No lessons seem to have been learned from these frightful experiences, for later statistics show no improvement. In the French Campaign in Madagascar in 1894 fourteen thousand men were sent to the front, of whom twenty-nine were killed in action and seven thousand perished from preventable disease. In the Boer War in South Africa the English losses from disease were simply frightful, greater than even our Civil War record.

But the crowning piece of imbecility was reserved for our war with Spain, where, in 1898, fourteen were needlessly sacrificed to ignorance and incompetency for every one who died on the firing line or from battle casualties.

The author points out how in Japan's war with China in 1894, the Japanese ratio of losses from disease was about the same as that suffered by American soldiers suffered in two of the wars cited above. The experience gained from that clash in Manchuria, however, was put to good use a decade later, and the Japanese army's ratio of combat casualties to those caused by disease turned around dramatically. Noting Japan's success, he writes, "Only one and two-tenths percent of the entire army died of sickness or disease. Only one and one-half died of gunshot wounds, although twenty-four percent were wounded . . . This record is, I believe, unparalleled and unapproached in the annals of war."

"Japan put into use the most elaborate and effective system of sanitation that has ever been practiced in war," he wrote. For instance, "every hospital throughout Japan, and every base and field hospital in Manchuria, has its bacteriological laboratory." The author praises the work done by "Japan's corps of trained experts with the microscope, that the dread phantom of disease might be intercepted." He describes the use of X-ray equipment at hospitals, and even portable X-ray machines in field hospitals.

In contrast, war correspondents recorded a statement by one of the Russian officers caught in the siege of Port Arthur: "Our principal enemies are the scurvy and 11-inch shells, which know no obstacle and against which there is no protection." (Eleven-inch shells were made possible by another Japanese scientific breakthrough, this time in gunpowder by Admiral Shimose Masachika; Shimose, like his compatriot Shiga, made it into *Webster's Dictionary.*)

Japan's early contact with bacteriological warfare was defensive. Seaman writes of the water sanitation methods which the Japanese practiced in an attempt to neutralize the problem that "the water supplies in the territory where the campaign was conducted had been left infected with the deadly germs of typhoid, dysentery, and cholera by the retreating Russians."

After the battle of Mukden, he wrote of sixty thousand Russian prisoners, many of them sick and wounded, taken by Japan. Another seventeen thousand sick and wounded were captured at Port Arthur. The American surgeon recorded how the Japanese cared for captured prisoners, taking careful case notes of their injuries and dressing their wounds, while the fleeing Russians left their dead and wounded so as to be able to retreat with maximum speed. Japan was in effect relieving the burden on the enemy hospitals. "This fact should be borne well in mind," Seaman wrote, "for should at a later date invidious comparisons be made regarding the low death-rate of the Russian wounded, it is Japan to whom the credit belongs. For it was under Japanese care that such a large percentage of them recovered."

British war correspondents also wrote of the wartime ethics of the Japanese. One account tells of Japanese patrols finding a Russian who was wounded in the eyes. The Japanese cleansed and dressed the wound, then returned the man to his own side. This was typical Japanese action in that war.

Most armies of the world considered the role of the medical corps something that began only after a soldier suffered sickness or injury. Japan took an opposite stand and used preventive bacteriology as part of tactical planning. "The army medical systems of the world were studied and a new one evolved, of which Japan may well be proud," Seaman writes, praising in particular a Japanese-developed portable water testing kit that technicians carried into the field in advance of the armies.

"The American Army," he wrote, "can never hope to emulate the Japanese until the time shall have arrived when, through the reorganization of its Medical Department, the surgeon shall have executive instead of merely advisory privileges in matters of hygiene and sanitation in barrack and field; and until the line officer shall display the same courtesy and respect to the medical expert as does his Japanese brother-in-arms."

Thus, by the turn of the century, Japanese military medicine and wartime bacteriology were the best in the world. Their standards, according to the American doctor, were far higher than those maintained by the United States and Great Britain, and medicine was treated by the Japanese as being equal in importance to guns and shells in contributing to military performance.

To address the problem of ingesting bacteria with food, the Japanese army issued creosote pills, an old standby formerly used in bronchial troubles, as a prophylactic measure. The army issued them to the soldiers with instructions to take one pellet after each meal. They tasted bad, though, and most of the pellets ended up in the fields. Japanese officers were concerned, and the problem of how to get the soldiers to take the creosote was sent back to headquarters in Tokyo to be discussed among top leaders. Sitting in on the conferences as a guest was a young American lieutenant, Douglas MacArthur, fresh out of West Point and son of the military attaché to Japan. The American's opinion was that soldiers were soldiers, and that there was no way to make the soldiers of any nation follow orders to swallow something that they didn't like.

The solution was found by a Japanese officer who suggested having the tins carry a message that "it is the will of the emperor that each soldier take this medicine after each meal." What followed is best described by MacArthur in his book *Reminiscences:* "The result was instantaneous. Not a pill was wasted. Nothing but death itself could stop the soldiers from taking the medicine."

The creosote was also given a new name which translates directly into "Subjugate Russia Pellets." It retained its name for a long time after the war, becoming a popular over-the-counter medicine for intestinal troubles. Then, after World War II, the Japanese Ministry of Health and Welfare ordered a change to eliminate the anti-Soviet connotation. A simple change of one of the ideographs in favor of one that resembled it left the pronunciation, s*eirogan,* unchanged, while turning the name of the medicine into a term with no particular meaning. Even today, *seirogan* can be found in any pharmacy in Japan.

The Japanese success in minimizing deaths from illness proved that they were correct in attaching equal priority to germs and bullets, and soon after the war's end, a Department of Field Disease Prevention was established. It was a natural outgrowth of the lessons learned in Manchuria and a peacetime continuation of what the American medical observer termed "the most elaborate and effective system of sanitation ever practiced in war." Commendable though this move was, though, it had its dark side. The original bacteriological aims of Japan were soon to be warped in the direction of causing, rather than preventing and curing, disease. And the fiber of the high morality of Japanese troops, praised by the American surgeon and foreign journalists and observers in Manchuria, would be shred and rewoven into racist ugliness at the hands of the Japanese military and medical elites.

Ishii Shiro

Ishii Shiro was born on June 25, 1892 in the village of Chiyoda, in an area about two hours' drive from what is today central Tokyo. His family was one of the wealthier ones in the region by village standards, with respectable land holdings that gave them the aura of rural aristocrats. This economic status earned respect and, more importantly, loyalty from the surrounding inhabitants. Ishii would put this loyalty to good use for himself in the coming years.

In 1916, Ishii entered Kyoto Imperial University. It was a prestigious establishment, and its medical department was especially known for its work in bacteriology. The "Schweitzer of Japan," Noguchi Hideyo, in addition to honors and awards he earned in the United States and Europe, received his Doctorate of Medicine from this university in 1911.

As a student, Ishii seemed to have had personality problems: more succinctly, he created problems for others. He was pushy, inconsiderate, and selfish. In harmony with these personality traits, he was also a ladder-climber. In a society where Confucian-rooted respect for superiors and a strong consciousness of hierarchy dictates boundaries of behavior, Ishii's forward drive ran roughshod over protocol.

Ishii felt a calling to the military, perhaps to serve his

country, but surely to advance his own goals of medical research. In 1920, he graduated university and enlisted in the army. Shortly thereafter, he was commissioned a lieutenant, and by the summer of 1922, he had managed to gain a transfer to the First Army Hospital in Tokyo. His fever for research was appreciated by his superiors, and two years later he was assigned to return to his alma mater for postgraduate work in bacteriology, among other fields.

During these days, he was a frequent visitor to the home of the school president, an affront to Ishii's university instructors in that he was socializing not only out of his own league, but theirs, as well. He eventually grew close enough to the top man at Kyoto Imperial University to marry his daughter. This marital link cemented his position with the university's medical research people and facilities; in a sense, thus, it also laid the beginnings of a foundation for his human experimentation in China.

Japan was a signatory to the Geneva Convention of 1925, which led to the prohibition of biological and chemical warfare. As a specialist in bacteria-related fields, Ishii actually found this development encouraging; he reasoned that if something were bad enough to be outlawed, then it must certainly be effective. In a way, Ishii's thoughts could be considered par for someone in a bureaucratic environment. Anyone familiar with life in a bureaucracy—especially a large and ponderous one—realizes that a large part of its total energy is expended to protect and enhance individual members' own roles in the organizational machinery.

Inspired by these developments, Ishii pressed for the establishment of a military arm whose activities centered around weapons based on biology. This was his field; the more important it became to the military, the greater his own importance would grow within the system. Financial considerations provided logic to support his cause. Compared with the costs of building, manning, and maintaining huge conventional forces, for example, bacteria and gas were far less expensive. Other advantages were to appear later, but the cost factor was a major selling point for Ishii in his appeals to the top levels of the Imperial Japanese Army.

Protection of one's own troops was still also part of the thinking about germs, a continuation of the military hygiene success of the Russo-Japanese War. While Ishii was a researcher at Kyoto, in fact, he was dispatched to help cure an epidemic that had broken out in a region of Japan, and during the course of his work he developed a water filtration system that could be transported along with troops. In general, however, he brought a new approach to military thinking about bacteriology. Why not enlist the "silent enemy" as a "silent ally"? He traveled frequently to Tokyo, still shaking hands with the top leaders of the army high command, still social-climbing, and still pleading his case for the development of bacteriological research as a weapon for offensive warfare.

The army had a policy of sending certain officers overseas to study foreign military facilities. Ishii left Japan in the spring of 1928 on a costly tour whose expenses came partly out of his own pocket. He spent more than two years visiting over twenty European countries, the United States, and Canada. Despite the fact that his own money was involved in funding his travel, however, his object was public-spirited: the furtherance of chemical and bacteriological warfare as Japanese military orthodoxy. He researched the history of gas weapons during World War I, and he studied what various countries were doing in the fields of bacteriological and gas warfare.

The climate he found in Japan when he returned in 1930 was more conducive to these thoughts than when he had left. Nationalism burned hotter. The old slogan of "a wealthy country, a strong army" that had attended the launch of the Meiji Restoration six decades earlier was echoing among the upper echelons of the military establishment. One of the men Ishii convinced to sponsor his efforts was the Minister of the Army, who coincidentally had the same family name as the president of Ishii's university. Araki Sadao—found guilty of overall conspiracy and waging war against China at the war crimes trials in Tokyo—was impressed with Ishii's findings and ambitions and set the army into action along the lines mapped out by Ishii.

Manchuria

The South Manchuria Railway was the Japanese-operated nerve center of the growing Manchurian economy, within which Japan had been developing a commercial and industrial base since 1904. It was also one of the best-run railways in the world. *Terry's Guide to the Japanese Empire,* a travel guide published in 1933, reports that

> Manchuria . . . with vast riches and a promising future, is rapidly being developed and modernized by the capable and progressive Japanese. A great factor in this development is the South Manchurian [sic] Railway, originally constructed by the Chinese Eastern Railway Company as a link in the trans-Siberian route, but acquired by Japan from Russia at the close of the Japan-Russia [sic] War. Under the present able Japanese management the rapidly spreading system has become one of the great high-

ways of the world, and it is as modern, as safe, and as dependable as the best American railway. Fast express trains, commodious sleeping cars and luxurious dining cars are features of the line, the employees of which speak English and Russian.

Apart from the transport services that it provided, the South Manchuria Railway also published English-language pamphlets for the major cities of Manchuria. They included maps, points of interest to tourists, and some historical background. The pamphlet for Mukden printed in 1933 contains an account of local history:

Manchurian Incident and North Barracks

At 10:30 P.M. on the 18th of Sept. 1931, the Manchurian Incident was started by the insolent explosion of the railway track at Liu-tiao kou between Mukden and Wen-kuan-tun stations of the South Manchuria Railway, which was executed by the Chinese regular soldiers. After the explosion, the Chinese soldiers attempted to flee themselves in the direction of the North Barracks, but just then they were found by the Japanese railway guards under Lieutenant Kawamoto, who were patrolling the place on duty. Suddenly the both sides exchanged the bullets and the Japanese made a fierce pursuit after them. On the next moment, the Chinese force of some three companies appeared from the thickly growed Kaolian [sorghum] field near the North Barracks, against which the Japanese opposed bravely and desperately, meantime despatching the urgent report to their commander. The skirmish developed speedily and the Japanese troop was compelled to make a violent attack upon the North

Barracks . . . After several hours of fierce battle, the barracks fell completely into the hand of the Japanese forces.

On the other hand, the Japanese regiment in Mukden rose in concert with the railway guards in the midnight of the same day and succeeded in occupying the walled town.

This "incident"—a pitched battle, actually—was no more than a Japanese ruse, used to justify occupying Mukden and moving on to a complete takeover of Manchuria. The real reasons behind the Japanese advance were a pair of developments in the region that had sounded warning bells to Japanese intent on retaining control of the area. First, China was showing trends toward unification under Nationalist leader Jiang Jieshi (Chiang Kaishek). Also, the Soviets were flexing their muscles and applying pressure from the north. The Kwantung Army made a move to strengthen its hold on Manchuria, with its wealth of coal, iron, an array of other ores, and oil.

Three days after the explosion at Mukden, supporting troops came in from Japan's colony of Korea, and in three months Japan had completely occupied Manchuria. Jiang was concentrating on establishing his influence over the rest of China at the time, and ordered a policy of nonresistance, leaving it for the ineffectual League of Nations to cope with Japan's invasion. Japan thereupon established a Manchuria-wide government, concocting an ironical euphemism by declaring the three eastern provinces an "independent" nation called Manzhouguo (Manchukuo). Henry Pu Yi, who had been emperor of the Manchu dynasty until 1912, when it abdicated its control of China, was pulled out of retirement to lead the new "nation." The Japanese gave him the title of "chief executive" to lend an illusion of historical legitimacy to the government.

With Japanese military control over Manchuria complete, the stage was set for the procurement of human specimens for the labs of Unit 731 and its associated organizations.

The Stage Is Set

As Japan continued expanding the breadth and depth of its power on the Asian mainland, Ishii Shiro's career also continued to advance apace. In 1932, an Epidemic Prevention Research Laboratory was set up within the army hospital in Tokyo, with Ishii in charge. The title of the laboratory was as euphemistic as Manzhouguo's "independence" and the "Great East Asian Coprosperity Sphere" banner under which Japan conquered neighboring countries. Prevention of disease in the Japanese military was still an objective of the research, but the center of gravity had shifted to development of bacteriological and chemical methods of warfare. This laboratory was Ishii's first major step in that direction.

Meanwhile, Japanese ascendancy in Manchuria was bringing the Japanese medical community closer to unprecedented opportunities for research. Ishii's goal of turning bacteria and gas into weapons of the Imperial Japanese Army would require comprehensive research, and animal research had serious limits in producing usable data. Growing control by Japan over Manchuria would provide research materials in the form of people, who could be plucked from the streets like lab rats. Toward the end of 1932, Ishii applied to the army to be sent to Manchuria to expand his research facilities. Then, the following year, Ishii's aggressive push for biological warfare research resulted in a grant of land and a building in Tokyo for his research. Coincidentally, this was the year in which Japan withdrew from the League of Nations, which had judged it in the wrong for its aggression against China. This severance of ties would be instrumental in freeing Japan's hands from any remaining constraints on the way she behaved in Asia.

The Japanese maintained control in Manchuria in a variety of ways. Emperor Pu Yi's police force, obedient to the commands of its Japanese puppeteers, was one law enforcement arm. In addition, there was a special police force which engaged in intelligence work but was also skilled in gaining confessions from suspected spies. Finally, perhaps the most terrifying group in the service of the Japanese Empire belonged to the elite group of military police known as the *kenpeitai.*

Substantial though Japanese capacity to maintain "public order" was, there was no lack of work for it. Opportunities to detain people constantly manifested themselves. The powers-that-were in Manchuria decreed anti-Japanese activity a cause for arrest, and the oppressive nature of the Japanese occupation created patriots who formed underground groups to oppose it. Groups and individuals kept up the anti-Japanese struggle long after official resistance had stopped, giving the Japanese an excuse to use them as research materials through all the years that the experiments continued. Some members of the resistance were captured and interrogated by the *kenpeitai,* then sent to the experimental labs.

Members of the *kenpeitai* were under orders of the army, and were specially selected for their rigid, oppressive, and unyielding personalities. They were given such jobs as catching spies and interrogating suspects, and were authorized to use torture if they were so inclined.

The *kenpeitai* spoke with daggers. They knew how to stare down a person, and how to use the voice to intimidate a suspect. People from an earlier era sometimes mentioned the fearsome way that these protectors of Japanese aims could shake a person with words, but even their descriptions failed to do justice to the reality. This is neither romanticizing nor exaggeration. Among the testimonies recorded in this book are those of former *kenpeitai* officers. One man, eighty years old, came out and told his audience, "I am a war criminal." For more than thirty minutes, that voice penetrated. In this case, it was turned against himself and the deeds he performed "for the country, for the emperor." Even at the age of eighty, that former *kenpeitai* officer was able to give an idea of what it must really have felt like to be stopped by himself or one of his comrades back in those dark days.

The *kenpeitai* served as a human materials procurement arm for Unit 731 and its associated outfits. A former *kenpeitai* officer from Dalian, Miou Yutaka, tells how the prisoners were handled: "We were the Special Handling forces of the *kenpeitai,* in charge of taking prisoners for the experiments of 731. We knew the prisoners would be used in experiments and not come back.

"We tied them with ropes around their waists, and their hands behind the backs. They couldn't move. We took them by train in a closed car, then the Unit 731 truck would meet us at the station. It was a strange truck—black with no windows. A strange-looking vehicle."

The gloomy, sealed freight cars to which Miou referred ran over the tracks of the South Manchuria Railway. They represented a much different side to the efficient railroad from the one that had impressed Terry the travel writer.

2
A New Type of Warfare

The Fortress/Bacteria Factory

The Manchurian city of Harbin was a railroad hub, and a multicultural, multiracial center of commerce, art, and music. It had been developed by the Russians just a few years before the Russo-Japanese War broke out. White Russians who had fled their country settled in Harbin. They were not well off, but at least they were not living in Russia, which seemed more important. Many of the women were beautiful, and a lack of other employment opportunities made them turn to prostitution. The racial and cultural mix made Harbin a fascinating city.

In 1932, a few months after Japanese troops moved into Harbin, Ishii and his associates followed them. Meanwhile, Japanese faced numerically superior Soviet troops along the Soviet-Manchurian border. An armed clash was expected, and Ishii planned to use his specialty to overcome his side's disadvantage.

Ishii's operations started out in Harbin with a few hundred men, but too many eyes in an urban center were not what he and his confederates wanted. To maintain their facade of respectability, they had the Harbin facility concentrate on the socially accepted area of vaccines and other "proper" medical research. Meanwhile, for the work they wanted kept completely quiet, they soon found another place about one hundred kilometers to the south. The ever-dependable and expanding South Manchuria Railway provided a means of transporting equipment and, more important, human lab materials.

The Japanese descended upon a poor neighborhood near an area known as Beiyinhe. There were about three hundred homes and shops there, with an extensive area of open land nearby to the south. Japanese troops came in and told the village headman that everyone had to clear out in three days; then Ishii and the army moved in. A large building of about one hundred rooms was kept for quarters while the facilities were being set up, and everything else was put to the torch. An area of five hundred square meters was designated a restricted military zone, and brick buildings started going up. The tract of land to the south was also forcibly appropriated and made into a Japanese military airport.

Chinese laborers were recruited and driven hard at wages low even by local standards. Their Japanese overseers argued that low pay was sufficient because the cost of living was low. But with large families the general rule in China, the pay for construction workers was barely enough to feed the mouths that depended on them.

With typical Japanese efficiency, the construction—comprising several hundred rooms—was finished in less than one year. Everything was veiled in secrecy. During construction, the laborers were under constant watch by Japanese guards, and their movements were limited. The number of laborers varied each day according to the work to be done. There were two sections to the complex. One contained offices, living quarters, dining areas, warehouses, and a parking lot. The other section contained the heart of the organization. In sequence as it concerned the victims, there were prisons, laboratories, and crematoria. There was also an area for munitions storage.

The area containing the lab was especially restricted to Chinese workers, but at times they had to enter to carry in materials or large boxes. In such cases, precautions bordering on the comical were taken to assure that the Chinese would see nothing. They were ordered to get under huge willow baskets that covered their bodies. They would then pick up their loads, be led in by Japanese guards, deposit their burdens, and be led out of the restricted area. Then they could come out from under the baskets.

The new facility was astounding to look at. It became known as Zhongma Fortress. (The character for fortress has also been translated as "castle," and it does, in fact, have that meaning in Japanese. In the original Chinese, however, it is applied to an entirely walled-in fortress city, a protection against enemy attacks. This is surely what the Japanese facility must have looked like to the outsiders.) A three-meter-high wall was topped with barbed wire and high-voltage electric wire. A twenty-four-hour guard was posted outside. Twin iron doors swung open to a drawbridge. The road in front of the facility was declared off-limits to the citizens, and people had to take a long way around to get to their destinations. Trains passing by on rails about a kilometer away were required to have their shades drawn.

One rumor told of a young boy who was curious about the Fortress and went out to have a look. His body was found the next day; he had been killed by gunfire. But even walls and guns could not keep rumors of cries of pain and anguish inside the Fortress from circulating through the village. And, by 1936, it was well known among the Chinese that this was not just a prison, but a production facility for bacteria, and a murder shop.

Some of the information on the facilities came from a shop owner in the area who went into the buildings after the Japanese had abandoned them. He described about thirty cells, and it seems that there were always about five to six hundred prisoners being held at any given time: the facility had the capacity to hold about one thousand. Another Chinese from the region was interviewed in more recent years about the Fortress:

> We heard rumors of people having blood drawn in there, but we never went near the place. We were too afraid.
>
> When construction started, there were about forty houses in our village, and a lot of people were driven out. About one person from each home was taken to work on the construction. People were gathered from villages from all around here, maybe about a thousand people in all.
>
> The only thing we worked on were the surrounding wall and the earthen walls. The Chinese that worked on the buildings were brought in from somewhere, but we didn't know where. After everything was finished, those people were killed.

The prisoners wore leg shackles and sometimes hand shackles, as well. They were given a substantial diet, their staples being rice or wheat, with meat or fish and sufficient vegetables, and at times even liquor. The purpose was to keep them in a normal state of health to yield useful data when they were subjected to the tests. One of these tests consisted of taking blood samples. At least five hundred cubic centimeters was drawn at two- to three-day intervals. Some of the victims became progressively debilitated and wasted. Still, the blood drainage continued. Careful records were kept, and these experiments smack more of a combination of professional curiosity than of actual science: a simple, childlike curiosity to see how far a human being can be squeezed of blood until death occurs. Not all were drained to the point of death, though. Many were injected with poison when they could no longer serve as lab materials. Sometimes, when a subject was too weak to offer physical resistance, he would be killed with a blow to the head with an axe. The brain might then be used for further research.

It is said that the life expectancy of prisoners at the Fortress was a maximum of one month.

An earlier experiment tried to determine how long a person could live on just water. Food was withheld from prisoners, and some were given only ordinary water, while others received only distilled water. They were observed as they wasted away and died.

By protecting its soldiers from disease in the Manchurian conflict thirty years earlier, Japan had earned international admiration by establishing itself as the world leader in military medicine. Now, the direction into which it channeled its medical energies had changed, and its ethics began to twist and mutate, as well. The leaders of Japan's military during the days of the Russo-Japanese War would undoubtedly have been appalled.

End of the Fortress

The escape from Zhongma Fortress in 1936 was a

combination of clever planning, daring, and coincidental help from a natural phenomenon. It involved some forty people who had been imprisoned at Harbin, then transferred to Zhongma for blood drawing.

A prisoner by the name of Li planned the jailbreak for the fifteenth day of the eighth month, a time of festivals marking autumn on the lunar calendar. The Japanese would be holding parties, and drinking, and prisoners would also be given special treats. Li knew that the Japanese guard would be bringing food and liquor, and after they were finished eating, the prisoners would hand the eating utensils out through the prison bars. Although the prisoners all had leg irons on, apparently their hands were free. When the utensils were handed back to the guard, Li grabbed his hand, dropped him with a blow to the head, grabbed the keys from around his waist, and opened the cells. Those who could, joined in the break. Others were too weak from repeated drawing of blood, and Li had no choice but to go on without them, leaving them to sure death while Li and his fellow prisoners seized their chance.

They ran out into the compound, and fortune smiled upon them with a heavy downpour that knocked out the electric power, deactivating the searchlights and electric fence. The escapees came to the wall and made a human ladder. Placing himself at the bottom, Li urged the others up and over. He was the only one left, and as the others ran as well as they could with their leg shackles, there were shots and one final shout from Li. At least, it was a more merciful death than his other option at the hands of the Japanese researchers.

Some ten of the escapees were gunned down. About twenty made it to the outside, but most of them either were killed or recaptured, or died from exposure, whose effects were compounded by the blood drawings. A few of the men came to a village and sought help from one of the residents. That person was interviewed in 1984 about the incident for a written account on the resistance movement. He recalls:

> That night I heard footsteps behind the house, then someone banging on the door. Outside there were seven men wearing leg shackles. My brother grabbed an axe to defend us, but when he heard their story he put down the axe, we took the men to a cave on the east side of the house, and we started breaking off the shackles. We were still working on them when the Japanese came to the edge of the village tracking down the escapees. So we thought of a way to free the men faster. First, we broke off a shackle from just one leg, so they could at least run while holding the other shackle. And then, they left the village.

Later, they managed to meet up with the other remaining escapees and all eventually teamed up with resistance fighters. But the secret of the Fortress was out. The Japanese had managed to keep things quiet for five years, but at last the time had come for a move.

Pingfang

The new site was closer to the city of Harbin, just a short hop away on the South Manchuria Railway. The Chinese called the location Pingfang; the Japanese reading of the same characters is Heibo. Between 1936 and 1938, a series of villages in the Pingfang area were seized by the Ishii organization in acts of military eminent domain. Hundreds of families were forced to sell their homes and land at the paltry sums decided upon by the Japanese Occupation. Forced evacuation ended generations of attachment to the lands and family graves. Often, land was confiscated at the end of the short growing season, and families had to move out without even being allowed to harvest their crops for the coming winter.

Surrounding buildings built by Chinese were limited to one story to keep out inquisitive eyes, and anyone—Japanese, Chinese, or otherwise—coming to Pingfang needed a pass. The airspace over the area was off-limits to all aircraft other than Japanese army planes; violators would be shot down. The headquarters was surrounded by a moat.

The Pingfang complex would grow into a sprawling, walled city of more than seventy buildings on a six-square-kilometer tract of land. Work was pushed ahead hard. During the months that construction was possible, a Japanese construction company, the Suzuki Group, worked round the clock in two shifts, day and night. At the coldest time of the year, the water, ground, and concrete all froze, bringing work to a halt. Winter was so harsh that the very first thing installed in the buildings, when they were still only shells, was the central heating system. The complex was probably finished around 1939, but the exact time remains uncertain, since construction teams were still working well after experiments started.

The prison blocks in the Pingfang compound were called "*ro* buildings." The term comes from the shapes of the Japanese syllabary character *ro* and the cell blocks, both of which are square. The Number 7 block held adult male prisoners, while Number 8 contained women and children. These prison blocks served the same purpose at Pingfang as cages for guinea pigs at conventional laboratories.

Cells were either single- or multiple-occupancy, and were arranged side by side, each with its window facing the corridor. An aperture that could be opened from the corridor was provided so that prisoners could extend their arms to receive injections or have blood samples drawn. The window and opening of each cell were located near the floor so that prisoners could extend their arms while in a reclining position; as the tests progressed, victims became unable to stand. Each cell had a flush toilet to maintain cleanliness, a wooden floor, and concrete walls heavier than necessary, probably built with recollections of the escape at Zhongma. Even walls between cells were thirty to forty centimeters thick. Central heating and cooling systems, and a well-planned diet, protected the health of the prisoners to ensure that the data they produced was valid. Poor living conditions or the presence of other disease germs could confuse results.

In all the gruesome professionalism that built the legacy of Unit 731, there was one touch of sardonic humor. As the massive Pingfang installation was under construction, local people began to ask what it was. The glib answer supplied was that the Japanese were building a lumber mill. Regarding this reply, one of the researchers joked privately, "And the people are the logs." From then on, the Japanese term for log, *maruta*, was used to speak of the prisoners whose last days were spent being torn apart or gassed by Japanese researchers. It is surprising how few Japanese realize the origin of this term, though the word itself never fails to come up when Unit

731 is discussed. The expression smacks of a racial attitude not even up to the level of disdain.

Pingfang was equipped for disposing of its consumed
human lab materials with three large incinerators—calling them crematoria would bestow undue dignity upon
them. A former member who assisted in the burning
commented, "The bodies always burned up fast because
all the organs were gone; the bodies were empty."

Ueda Yataro was a researcher working under a leader
of one of the teams into which researchers and assistants
were organized. He later woke up to the aberrant thinking which led him and others to participate in the activities of Unit 731. He recorded his experiences,
disjointedly, in pages of handwritten notes. The following is an excerpt about one of the research projects that
he worked on. His "material" was in a cell with four other
maruta.

He was already too weak to stand. The heavy leg
irons bit at his legs. When he moved, they made a
dull, clanking sound. His fellow cellmates sat around
him, and watched him. Nobody spoke. The water
in the toilet was running with an ominous sound.

In the corridor outside the cell, the guards stood
with their pistols strapped on. The commander of
the guards was there also. The man's screams of
death had no effect on them. This was an everyday
occurrence. There was nothing special.

To these guards, the people in here have already
lost all rights. Their names have been exchanged
for just a number written across the front of their
shirts and the name m*aruta*. They are referred to
only as "*Maruta* Number X." They are counted not

as one person or two persons but "one log, two logs." We are not concerned with where they are from, how they came here.

The man looked like a farmer, covered with grime. He was wasting away, and his cheekbones protruded. His eyes glared out from the dirt and the tattered cotton clothes he was wrapped in.

The team leader was fully pleased with yesterday's results. We never had such a typical change in blood picture and rate of infection, and I was eagerly looking forward to see what changes would be present in today's blood sample. With high hopes, I came to the Number 7 cell block with the armed guards at my side. The *maruta* I was working on was on the verge of death. It would be disastrous if he died. Then I would not be able to get a blood sample, and we would not obtain the important results of the tests we had been working on.

I called his number. No answer came. I motioned through the window at the other four prisoners to bring him over. They sat there without moving. I screamed abusively at them to hurry up and bring him over to the window. One of the guards pulled out a gun, aimed it at them, and screamed in Chinese. Resigned, they gently lifted up the other man and brought him over to the window. More important to me than the man's death was the blood flowing in the human guinea pig's body at the moment just before his death.

His hand was purplish and turning cold. He put his arm through the opening. I was elated. Filled with a sense of victory and holding down my inexpressible excitement, thinking forward to how the team leader would be waiting for these results, I reached for the hypodermic.

I inserted the needle into the vein. It made a dull sound. I pulled the red-black blood into the hypodermic. Three cubic centimeters . . . five cubic centimeters . . . His face became paler. Before, he'd been moaning; now he could not even moan. His throat was making a tiny rasping sound like an insect. With resentment and anger in his eyes, he stared at me without even blinking. But that did not matter. I obtained a blood sample of ten cubic centimeters. For people in laboratory work, this is ecstasy, and one's calling to his profession. Showing compassion for a person's death pains was of no value to me.

At the lab, I processed the blood sample quickly and then went back to look into the cell. His face occasionally twitched. His breath became shallower, and he went into his death throes.

The other four men in the cell, who had the same fate waiting for them, could not contain their anger. They took water and poured it into the mouth of the dead man.

This way, an irreplaceable life is trifled with to take the place of a guinea pig, and the result is one sheet of graph paper.

Four or five soldiers, with drawn guns, opened the door to the cell. It made a heavy sound. They dragged the dead man out into the corridor and loaded him onto a hand cart. The other four men, knowing what their fate would be tomorrow, could not hold down the anger in their eyes as they watched their dead companion leave.

The hand cart disappeared in the direction of the dissection room with the tall chimney looming above.

Human experimentation gave researchers their first chance to actually examine the organs of a living person at will to see the progress of a disease. Vivisection was a new experience for the doctors of Japan. One former unit member explained that "the results of the effects of infection cannot be obtained accurately once the person dies because putrefactive bacteria set in. Putrefactive bacteria are stronger than plague germs. So, for obtaining accurate results, it is important whether the subject is alive or not."

The research methods in Manchuria allowed doctors to induce diseases and examine their effects on organs at the first stages. Researchers worked with interpreters to ask about emerging symptoms, and took subjects out of cells at what they judged to be the time for optimum results. Anesthesia was optional. According to a former unit member: "As soon as the symptoms were observed, the prisoner was taken from his cell and into the dissection room. He was stripped and placed on the table, screaming, trying to fight back. He was strapped down, still screaming frightfully. One of the doctors stuffed a towel into his mouth, then with one quick slice of the scalpel he was opened up."

Even with the intestines and organs exposed, a person does not die immediately. It is the same physical situation as ordinary surgery under anesthesia in which a person is operated on and restored. Witnesses at vivisections report that the victim usually lets out a horrible scream when the cut is made, and that the voice stops soon after that. The researchers then conduct their examination of the organs, remove the ones that they want for study, then discard what is left of the body. Somewhere in the process, the victim dies, through blood loss or removal of vital organs.

A very brief video testimony was provided by Kurumizawa Masakuni. He was advanced in age and weak at the time of the interview, and only photographs of him appeared on screen. His voice was almost inaudible. He spoke of the time he was working on a woman victim who had awakened from anesthesia while being vivisected. The woman interviewing him asked what happened.

"She opened her eyes."

"And then?"

"She hollered."

"What did she say?"

Kurumizawa could not answer, then began weeping feebly and murmured, "I don't want to think about it again."

The interviewee apologized, waited a few seconds, and tried again for an answer. He gave it through sobs.

"She said, 'It's all right to kill me, but please spare my child's life.'"

Four months after this interview, Kurumizawa died.

A similar incident is reported in Part 2 of this book. There is no way of knowing whether these two reports refer to the same episode. Women were captured and experimented upon, and a large number of babies were born in captivity. Some were born to women who had been brought in while pregnant. Others were born to women who became pregnant in forced sex acts during tests investigating the transmission of venereal disease.

There are accounts of experiments being carried out on mothers and children. The gas chamber was one venue for these tests. Also, Part 2 of this book includes an account of three mothers with children used in an air drop of pathogens. It is conceivable that more than one mother voiced, as a last wish on the vivisection table, the wish to let her child live. No one ever did. The researchers wanted their data.

Two modes of transportation were important to the unit's functioning. The railroad, the lifeline of Japan's industrial venture in Manchuria, was one indispensible part of the Ishii organization. Windowless cars of prisoners were carried from point of capture or imprisonment to a railroad siding at the Pingfang prison labs. One rare eyewitness account of an unloading told of prisoners bound with hands behind them and laid head-to-foot on a flatbed wagon for transfer from the freight car to the prison cells. After unloading their cargo, trains would return empty. It was an almost invisible way of shifting people out of circulation.

The other important artery was the airfield built off to one side of the building complex within the unit grounds. Conscious as Ishii was of his own prospects for personal advancement, he made frequent trips to Tokyo's Army Medical College to present his work. The materials for presentation included more than graphs and drawings; he also displayed human specimens. The specimen jars themselves were made in Manchuria by a European-trained Japanese, and specimens were regular passengers on the flights from Pingfang to Tokyo. Some vessels contained extremities, specimens of arms, legs, and feet. Other jars contained organs. Some were heads. Still others were whole-body specimens. With this air connection putting Ishii a couple of hours away from his Tokyo base, Pingfang became a virtual specimen-supply annex to the Tokyo medical school. Return flights to

Pingfang, for their part, carried supplies, including cages of rats.

Doctors who knew the situation at the time have commented that this Pingfang-Tokyo air corridor was run on a very regular basis. Through this channel, the results of experiments came to Japan in the form of new bacteria, as well as preserved specimens of human subjects who had died from a range of artificially induced pathological conditions. These materials were made available not just to the army hospital, but to researchers throughout Japan. This gave universities the chance to study diseases not then in Japan, such as plague, cholera, and epidemic hemorrhagic fever (EHF). In this way, Unit 731 was performing the service of human experimentation for the entire Japanese medical community— civilian and military, public and confidential.

A worker in materials procurement at the army hospital named Amano Ryuji comments on both aspects of the two-way traffic. "It was simple to bring those rats to Manchuria by plane. The plane brought the specimens of human bodies and parts into Tokyo for presentation and study, and carried rats back on the return trip. I saw large numbers of specimens of body parts at the Tokyo lab. Those are the bones that were dug up in Shinjuku [near the former site of the Army Medical College, some fifty years later]. I think that there are more bones there than were found. If someone looked they would discover more."

The scope of the service comes into sharper focus when the dispersion of the organization is considered. In addition to the Pingfang central unit, there were units set up in Beijing, Nanjing, Guangzhou, and Singapore. In addition, some of these units had their own branch units.

The total number of personnel reached some twenty thousand people. Human specimens were known to come to the Pingfang headquarters from other units, and since different units more or less specialized in certain areas of research, it can be assumed that sibling units supplied pathological specimens not available at Pingfang. All of these were candidates for the trip to Tokyo and the Japanese world of medical research. Meanwhile, the windowless trains and cars kept rolling, and the incinerators kept smoking.

Satellite Facilities

While the Pingfang facility was to become synonymous with human experimentation, the actual Unit 731 designation did not come into use until August 1941. It became a type of generic term, referring not only to the Pingfang-based unit, but also encompassing its sibling units in other locations, and even its predecessors. All units and facilities were coordinated by the Epidemic Prevention Research Laboratory in Tokyo. Some of the more important of the less well known facilities are described here.

Anda

This was an open-air testing ground one hundred twenty kilometers from Pingfang, about three hours by road. It was used for outdoor tests of plague, cholera, and other pathogens in experimental biological warfare bombs, and other methods of exposing human beings to pathogenic substances in open-air situations.

Tests generally used from ten to forty people at a time, with subjects tied to crosses in circles of various sizes.

The tests involved an element of trial and error, and comparing results obtained from differently sized circles enabled researchers to determine ranges of effectiveness at various distances from the points where projectiles struck or infected insects were released. When biological warfare bombs were tested, each *maruta* was protected with headgear and a metal plate hung from the neck to cover the front part of the body. These protective devices prevented death or serious injury that would make it imposssible to obtain the needed data. Arms and legs were left exposed, so that they could be bitten by the disease-carrying insects. In some tests, subjects were tied to vertical boards that were anchored into the ground at various distances and patterns from points of release. Careful notes were made of wind and atmospheric conditions, and each person was marked with a number on his or her chest during each test for easy tracking of human specimens.

Xinjing

Under veterinarian Wakamatsu Yujiro, Unit 100 in Xinjing (present-day Changchun), concentrated its research on pathogens effective against domesticated animals. The horses and edible animals of the Soviet and Chinese armies were the targets of this research. Unit 100 was also a bacteria factory, producing large quantities of glanders, anthrax, and other pathogens.

Sabotage was another focus of the operations here, and one experiment entailed mixing poisons with food to study their effects on subjects and to gain knowledge of appropriate dosages for various toxins. Additionally, extensive areas of land were cultivated for research into chemicals for crop destruction.

Guangzhou

The Guangzhou unit has been mentioned in documentary films and written reports, though its activities have not been fully clarified, nor had its existence even been decisively proven. In late October 1994, a private research mission from Japan went to Guangzhou to investigate the possibility of Japanese biological warfare activity there. They also located a former unit member in Japan, who provided them with additional evidence of a germ warfare unit's having been in Guangzhou.

They learned from the former member that the unit, called Nami Unit 8604, was headquartered at Zhongshan Medical University. The building stands today very much as it did then, and information gleaned from Chinese government records and inhabitants of the area show that Unit 8604 was established in 1938. It was staffed by several hundred personnel.

The *Japan Times* of November 9, 1994, reported on a seventy-seven-year-old former unit member, Maruyama Shigeru, who said that one experiment involved starving prisoners to death. This test would appear to be similar to the tests done at Harbin to determine how long a person can continue living on water alone.

The former unit member also stated that a large number of Chinese refugees from Hong Kong died after they were given water containing typhus-causing bacteria provided by the Army Medical College in Tokyo. In addition, Maruyama talked of seeing victims being operated on almost every day. He recalled that many bodies were stored in the basement of the building.

The Guangzhou unit, according to Maruyama, also raised rats for experiments in spreading plague. This addition to the Ishii organization's litany of experiments with rats and plague serves as yet further evidence that plague was high on the list of priorities in Japan's design for conquest by disease.

A Chinese witness at Guangzhou volunteered that there was a pond of chemicals inside the university compound that was used to dissolve the bodies of the victims. It can be inferred that since this unit was established inside a previously existing medical facility, it did not have the incineration capabilities of the Harbin and Pingfang locations, which were custom-built and equipped with the facilities necessary for disposing of large numbers of bodies.

Beijing

After the Japanese evacuation at the end of the war, Chinese locals entered the facilities of Beijing-based Unit 1855 for a look behind its secrets. The building still exists, and a Japanese documentary program's video camera followed a bacteriologist who had been posted at the facility, as he described what had gone on in the days when he and his colleagues had worked there. "This is where large numbers of test tubes were all lined up on shelves," he narrated. "Each test tube was identified by a label showing what kind of bacteria it contained. Six of them contained plague germs."

Unit 1855 had a branch in Chinan that was a combination prison and experiment center. On the same documentary, a Korean man, Choi Hyung Shin, told about his experience there as an interpreter.

Choi first went to China when he was sixteen years old to attend school. After the Japanese annexation of Korea in 1910, there were attempts to replace Korean culture with Japanese culture, and all children received a Japanese education. Choi's trilingual ability made him useful to the Japanese doctors. Korean immigrants to China were among the victims of human experimentation, and Choi's interpreting between the Japanese researchers and their Korean and Chinese test subjects was vital to the acquisition of proper research data. He worked at the branch for almost two years during 1942 and 1943.

> When I first arrived there, some one hundred prisoners were already in the cells. Whenever the Japanese doctors made contact with the people being tested, they always did it through an interpreter.
>
> The test subjects were infected with plague, cholera, and typhus. Those not yet infected were kept in different rooms. There were large mirrors in the rooms with the subjects so that those undergoing testing could be observed better. I spoke with the prisoners using a microphone and looking through the glass panel, interpreting the questions from the doctors: "Do you have diarrhea? Do you have a headache? Do you feel chilly?" The doctors made very careful records of all the answers.
>
> With the typhus test, ten people were forced to drink a mixture of the germs, and five of them were administered vaccine. The two groups were kept separate from each other. The doctors watched them closely and questioned them through my interpretation, recording the answers. The vaccine proved effective with all five to whom it was administered. The other five suffered horribly.
>
> In the plague tests, the prisoners suffered with chills and fever, and groaned in pain . . . until they died. From what I saw, one person was killed every day.

Constantly forced to be part of the morbid business of

infection and killing, Choi faked appendicitis, which got him sick leave from his job and a chance to escape. Unfortunately, he was caught by *kenpeitai* officers and given the water torture with hot peppers mixed into the water. This caused him permanent lung damage, and he has been in and out of the hospital for the past fifty years.

Singapore

In September 1991, journalist Phan Ming Yen of the Singapore *Straits Times* broke the story that it had apparently been confirmed that a Japanese biological warfare installation—rumored but not proven to have existed—had operated in Singapore. He wrote his story after locating a man who claimed to have worked in the lab as a youth. Phan announced that "a Singapore connection has been mentioned fleetingly in some accounts, but no concrete evidence has been cited until now.

"Confirmation of the Singapore secret laboratory was made following a *Straits Times* interview with Mr. Othman Wok, sixty-seven, former minister for social affairs, who said he worked as an assistant in the laboratory for over two years during the Japanese Occupation." According to the *Straits Times* article, the research unit, code-named Oka 9420, was situated in a building now occupied by the Drug Administration Division of the Ministry of Health, and "local historians contacted were unaware of the existence of the laboratory.

Singapore was captured by the Japanese in February 1942. Several months later, Othman, then seventeen years old, found himself looking for employment in the occupied land, and his uncle, who worked in a Japanese-run laboratory, provided a recommendation that enabled Mr. Othman to get a job. His unwitting contribution to Japan's biological warfare program thus began.

Seven Chinese, Indian, and Malay boys working in the lab were all assigned the task of picking fleas from rats and putting them into containers. The article quotes Othman Wok as saying, "It was an unforgettable experience. It was the first time that I was doing something which made me feel like a medical student."

Some forty rat catchers, apparently Japanese soldiers, would comb Singapore for the rodents and bring their haul into the lab. The rats would then be put to sleep with chloroform, and the boys would work at pulling the fleas from their bodies with pincers. Then the fleas were placed into containers with water, which prevented them from jumping around, and from there the Japanese staff took over. According to Othman, test tubes were prepared with one flea in each. The rats were injected with plague pathogens, their bellies were shaved, and the test tubes were inverted over the shaved area, allowing the fleas to feed on the rats and become plague carriers. "All this work was done by the Japanese in the same room where I worked," Othman recounted.

The infected fleas were then transferred to kerosene cans which contained sand, dried horse blood, and an unidentified chemical. They were left to breed for about two weeks. Finally, the adult fleas and their offspring, all infected with plague, were transferred to flasks and shipped out. Concerning their destination, Mr. Othman said, "A driver who drove the trucks which transported the fleas to the railway station said that these bottles of fleas were sent off to Thailand." This information supports assertions that a Unit 731 branch operated in "neutral" Thailand, as well.

The Singapore operation was veiled in the same secrecy that covered other installations. "During the two years I was working there," Mr. Othman is quoted as saying, "I never knew the actual purpose of my work. We were too afraid to ask."

Without being told so, the boys knew that they were working with danger. Everybody had to wear white overalls, rubber gloves and boots, and white headgear. On one occassion a rat bit through the rubber glove of a Japanese staffer, and the man died. Another time, an Indian boy working there was bitten on the finger by a rat, but he was saved by being rushed to the hospital and having the tip of the finger amputated.

Othman left the laboratory in late 1944 for another job. After the war, he read of a Japanese biological warfare attack on Chongqing using fleas, and he stated in the article that "the thought that I could have been involved in something related to that still troubles and worries me." In the years intervening between the end of the war and his speaking to the *Straits Times*, he never spoke of his employment at Unit 9420.

In Japan, historian Matsumura Takao of Keio University credited the information from the former official with filling the gap between what had been strongly suspected about the Singapore operation and the lack of substantive proof. He also set about on his own search for information concerning the laboratory. He located the former head of the laboratory and got a story, albeit with credibility gaps. Phan of the *Straits Times* then followed up on his coverage in the newspaper's November 11, 1991 issue with a second piece on the issue. In an article headlined "Germ lab's head says work solely for research, vaccines . . . But Japanese professor sceptical about his claim," Phan followed the progress of Professor Matsumura's investigation into the issue, while also giving space to the former laboratory administrator's rebuttal.

The story gave the Japanese government a problem, and it issued the predictable and well-worn denial. Concerning this response, Phan wrote that "the Japanese government responded, saying that it had no records of such a laboratory—a claim which contrasted with those in U.S. Army documents which mentioned its existence." The documents of course are those which U.S. military authorities gathered from interviews with Unit 731 leaders forty-five years earlier, which made some passing mention of a Singapore unit.

The former head of the Singapore facility was "a retired doctor in his early eighties who refused to be identified." According to the article, "he said he was transferred to Singapore a week after the island was occupied in February, 1942 from the main branch of . . . Unit 731 in Harbin, Manchuria. Singapore was the headquarters of the Japanese Southern Army and the base to supply material to the war front. To prevent the outbreak of diseases in the city, strict bacteriological checks on water supply and fresh food were carried out." The retired doctor mentions soldiers catching rats in the city and conducting experiments with them, and comments, "Such behavior must have seemed odd to the people there and thus caused misunderstanding."

Did the people misunderstand? Or did they, in fact, understand all too well? The former laboratory chief talks of the large scale on which his facility operated—it employed all of one thousand members—and the fact that it was had been set up by people brought into Singapore by Naito Ryoichi, a prominent Unit 731 officer who later played an important role in the outfit's first negotiations with American occupation forces.

Matsumura's counterargument concerning the benign role allegedly played by the Singapore unit was also carried in the same newspaper: "The other four branches of the unit at Harbin, Guangzhou, Beijing and Nanjing were involved in the manufacture of germ warfare weapons. It would seem strange if the branch in Singapore was not involved in similar activities." More pointedly, he adds that it seemed odd to set up a laboratory for research on a disease in a place in which there was no epidemic. And he notes that the head of the lab, Naito, and other members had all come to Singapore after working in Harbin, where biological warfare weapons were manufactured.

In February 1995, a documentary on an Asahi Broadcasting Company program interviewed a former member, Takayama Yoshiaki, of the Singapore unit. His account of what he did in Singapore falls into the pattern of Japan's methodology for creating plague as a weapon. He recalls, "We raised fleas in oil cans. Then, the infected rats were put into mesh enclosures, and lowered into the cans. The fleas would bite the rats, and the fleas became infected."

The discovery of these facts regarding the Singapore unit throws light upon the geographical extent of Japan's biological warfare ambitions.

Hiroshima

The charming island of Okunoshima lies just a few minutes by boat from the port city of Hiroshima. In 1929, a factory on the island started producing poison gas for chemical warfare. A small museum has been established near the remains of the factory to remind people of what went on here. The curator is a former worker in what was a highly secretive, dangerous operation. Photos show the scars and disfigurements suffered by the workers.

The island's history as a center for chemical warfare production dates back to 1928, when the installation there engaged in production of mustard gas on an experimental basis. Equipment was imported from France, and workers were brought in from nearby rural communities on the Japanese mainland.

With the expansion of the war in the latter part of the 1930s, the Hiroshima plant increased production. Types of gases produced over the factory's lifetime include yperite, lewisite, and cyanogen. So important—and confidential—was the work done at the island that it actually disappeared from Japanese maps as the army moved more aggressively into China.

The workers themselves were ordered to the same secrecy as Unit 731 personnel. And, as with Unit 731, the Japanese government has shown a deep reluctance to admit that anything untoward went on at Okunoshima. For a long time, the government refused to acknowledge responsibility for assisting former workers at the factory there. Finally, it granted some of them recognition as poison gas patients and allowed them compensation, if far from sufficient. For all the destitution and respiratory and other health problems these people have suffered, though, they are comparatively lucky: many of their colleagues died before the government moved to grant them any form of assistance at all.

The plant on Okunoshima supplied some of the gas used in the human experimentation in Manchuria. A reported two million canisters of poison gas abandoned in China by the Japanese army has been a constant bone of contention between the two countries. China has been asking for its removal, while the Japanese government has appeared to be waiting for it simply to go away on its own. Finally, some fifty years after the end of World War

II, Japan is reacting to pressure, time, and perhaps the incentive of benefits perceived to be had from good relations with an economically booming China. At last, the abandoned gas weapons are scheduled for deactivation. Poison gas does not seem to fit in well with a booming, mercantilistic atmosphere.

Ties to the Civilian Sector

The massive scale of the new buildings and grounds was not the only major change concerning Ishii Shiro's work when Unit 731 moved to Pingfang. The change in venue brought about a drastic revision in organization, as well. The first fortress/bacteria factory had been staffed only by military doctors and technicians. Now, however, Ishii aimed to move on from what had been a restricted exercise in military medicine, and involve the entire Japanese medical community. In order to attain this objective, Ishii once again needed to cash in on his talent for manipulation, this time to convince researchers to leave the security of their labs and join him in Manchuria. In the final analysis, Ishii's talent as an organizer would be evaluated as being greater than his research ability, despite the knack for invention testified to by his water purification systems and biological warfare bombs.

He went back to his alma mater in Kyoto, to Tokyo Imperial University, and to other leading medical universities, and coaxed professors and researchers to come to Manchuria. Attracted by the lure of expanding their research possibilities, some researchers went themselves, while others sent their students. The students would write up their research, then send it back to their professors, who would then use the data to prepare their own reports and advance themselves in the medical community. In defense of some of the people recruited, it must be acknowledged that not all of them knew what they were getting into and were themselves used by Ishii and his henchmen. There were also students who were pressured by their professors to go work with Ishii's organization. Defying a professor in Japan's strict academic hierarchy was (and remains even today) equivalent to career suicide.

The degree of civilian involvement in the human-experimentation units has been a matter of discussion in Japan for some time, but a recent statement by a former unit member throws past estimates into a new light. In 1994, a former unit member by the name of Okijima, then seventy-eight years old, offered the following comment on the personnel of Unit 731: "Some things have to be corrected. There were no soldiers at Unit 731. They were all civilian employees."

"All" may be an exaggeration since the top leaders— Ishii, Lieutenant General Kitano Masaji, who took over charge of the unit in 1942, and some others—were in the military. Okishima's statement does imply, however, that there were more civilian researchers than conventional accounts would lead us to believe. It has also been repeatedly noted that many researchers came to Manchuria for a limited time, performed their work, and then were replaced by others in a constant cycle. This rotation would suggest the presence of civilian researchers who would come from their respective universities, work on particular projects, then return home with their results.

Like soldiers, civilians also had a variety of ranks, spanning the hierarchical spectrum from the equivalent of common grunts, up to generals. University researchers made up the majority of civilian employees at the Ishii organization, and their statuses were determined by the universities from which they hailed. Those from the elite Tokyo University and Kyoto University held the highest grades. (The Tama Unit in Nanjing, in particular, had deep ties with Tokyo University.) Each university researcher had his own lab when he was at the unit, and directed the course of the project he was working on.

Medical professionals were not the only civilians to be called into duty with Unit 731. The wartime militarization of Japan extended even down to the level of children in grade school. For instance, teachers were ordered to scan students' compositions for signs of anti-war sentiments among the parents. If any such tendencies surfaced, they would be reported to the school principal, and from there to the police, who would investigate the parents. Teachers were also used to whip up patriotic feelings in their students, and encourage them to join the Youth Corps.

Young and impressionable, inculcated with the values of obedience to authority and emperor worship, the Youth Corps served an important role in Ishii's organization. Boys from fifteen through seventeen years of age who eventually ended up at Unit 731 usually had no idea of what they were headed for. Many were sidetracked from their intended fields of activity to serve in Pingfang as assistants to researchers. They were put through a tough, accelerated schedule of study in biology, math, bacteriology, and foreign languages. Their work at the unit included carrying organs freshly removed from victims from the dissection rooms to labs where preservation or further research would take place. These services made the Youth Corps members important witnesses in later years. While they had not yet acquired the wisdom to comprehend the full significance or extent of the experiments in progress, they understood a great deal for their age. They were looked to as disciples to carry on Japan's future scientific and military adventures. They were the youngest members to witness the happenings, and many of them are still here today and have provided crucial testimony.

How was it possible for someone to bring together so large a number of scientific researchers, as Ishii did? Some critics say that the demand from the medical community was there, and Ishii answered it. The data traffic was organized so that when a researcher completed an experiment, its results were announced to Ishii. If a new substance were developed, for example, that report would be brought to him in his capacity as the representative of the Epidemic Prevention Research Laboratory. The report or substance (in the case of a vaccine, etc.) would then be sent to another Ishii unit for testing. If a professor were in Japan and his student were experimenting in China, the professor would receive the work of that student through the Epidemic Prevention Research Laboratory in Tokyo. If the results were incomplete, this information would be channeled back through the Epidemic Prevention Research Laboratory, and the experiments would continue further. In this way, the Epidemic Prevention Research Laboratory was a coordinating body that tied in civilian research in Japan with military research in Japan and overseas. Japanese military aggression made the human experimentation possible; the Japanese medical community was the silent inquisitor.

Ishii's Battlefield Debut

Despite the fact that Ishii's organization was officially a water purification and disease prevention unit, these missions were a distant second priority for it. Japanese military medicine had grown away from its Russo-Japanese War heritage. In 1937, however, it took a turn back toward its roots—protection of Japanese troops from disease—when, during some fighting, Japanese soldiers drank from a creek and many cases of cholera broke out. It was said that, because of the diarrhea, very few soldiers were fighting with their pants on. The Japanese suspected that the Chinese had contaminated the stream.

Ironically, Ishii, virtually all of whose career had been devoted to developing offensive biological warfare, played an important role in this brief return to defensive medicine. An invention of his, a portable water filtering system, was finally allowed to accompany the troops. The machine was a cylindrical mechanism about one meter in length and forty-five centimeters in diameter. Water was fed in at one end, and a hand crank forced the water under pressure through a filtering system of unglazed diatomite. This was the same material used in his bombs.

Ishii's device had not proven effective against cholera germs in tests to date, but the sense of urgency brought about by the combination of increasing numbers of incapacitated soldiers and Ishii's typical heavy-handed insistence convinced the army to put his system into operation. Five trucks carrying water filtration units and a team of about two hundred men started supplying drinking water to the Japanese fighting men, and, for reasons that remain unclear, cholera cases dropped sharply. Ishii was decorated and received a monetary award for his contribution to Japan's fighting forces. The praise he received caught the attention of American intelligence personnel who were interested in why the work of an army doctor was so highly regarded. This was the first time Ishii's name came to the attention of the American military.

Shortly thereafter, Ishii would be unleashed to pursue

his real calling, offensive biological warfare. In 1938 and 1939, the Soviet and Japanese armies clashed in two full-scale encounters at the Manzhouguo border and former Mongolian border. The latter battle, which came to be known as the Nomonhan Incident, resulted in an overwhelming defeat of the Japanese forces. The clash, which saw the first field operation of the biological warfare unit, occurred in a desert region where water was scarce. Bidding a quick adieu to the water purification role that he had helped play in China, Ishii was undoubtedly more at home with his new mission: plans now called for his unit to cause epidemics by poisoning the water supply of the enemy.

In 1989, a journalist for the *Asahi* newspaper held a meeting with three former Youth Corps members of Unit 731. It was a quiet, private affair covered in the newspaper's August 24 edition with the headline "Typhoid Germs Thrown Downstream at Nomonhan Incident: Three Men Formerly Connected with Ishii Unit Testify After Fifty Years." The article reported their stating that "with our own hands, we threw large quantities of intestinal typhoid bacteria into the river during the Nomonhan Incident." But the tactic produced more questions than results.

According to the recollections of the three men, the use of typhoid germs was initiated by the Ishii unit after the Japanese sustained a heavy attack. By the latter part of August, it was clear that Japan's Manchurian army would be defeated, and the biological warfare operation would appear to have been undertaken out of desperation. According to the account in the article,

> the upper reaches of the of the river were not far from the Japanese army camp. [Group Leader]

Yamamoto's plan was to throw the pathogens into the river so that they would travel downstream to the Russo-Mongol army and infect the soldiers. We loaded the pathogens into two trucks and headed for the dumping area. There were fourteen or fifteen of us, including the leader. Over the next few days, we made two attempts to reach the river, but couldn't make it because of heavy Russian artillery fire and the trucks' getting bogged down in soft ground. Then, on the third try we made it to the river. It was around early September. The location was one or two hours by truck from our camp, and we traveled at night, without lights, to a point near the dumping site. The pathogens were stored in twenty-two or twenty-three 18-liter oil drums. The cans were tied with straw rope, and we carried one in each hand. We crossed over swampy ground to the riverbank, watching the Soviet-Mongolian army's signal flares shooting up overhead from the opposite side. The pathogens were cultured in a vegetable gelatin. We opened the lids, and poured the jelly-like contents of the cans into the river. We carried the cans back with us so we wouldn't leave any evidence.

One of the men added that, at the time, he did not know what the pathogens were, but some time later, a hygiene specialist from a special operations team died in a hospital from typhoid, and he assumed that it was the same disease as the germs he had carried in the Nomonhan Incident.

The *Asahi* reporter also spoke with an instructor of military history at the Japanese Defense Agency who had known the leader of that action, Lieutenant Colonel

Yamamoto, after the war. The instructor told of Yamamoto's receiving the Order of the Golden Kite for meritorious service at the time of the incident.

The *Asahi* article was capped off with a comment by Professor Tsuneishi Keiichi, a professor at Kanagawa University and probably Japan's leading expert on Unit 731: "The use of BW at the Nomonhan Incident is also recorded in testimony at the Khabarovsk military trials in 1949. But if intestinal typhoid germs are dumped into a river, they will become ineffective almost immediately. The Ishii unit people surely knew that. Rather than actually conducting biological warfare, it seems more likely that it was a method of gaining publicity for the unit, as well as a drill. But the Nomonhan Incident was definitely the first use of BW by the Japanese army."

The Epidemic Prevention and Water Supply Department was responsible for sanitary work wherever Japanese troops were in China. According to post-World War II testimony by Ishii to Lieutenant Colonel Arvo Thompson of the U.S. Army in 1946, Japan's initiation of biological warfare was defensive. There was always the danger that Chinese troops would themselves employ bacteriological tactics, and so the Japanese had no choice but to expand the scope of their biological countermeasures in step with the military operations then underway.

Looking at the record of Ishii's fascination with biological warfare from his European tour, and his aggressive salesmanship of it to the army upper echelons, it seems clear that there was nothing defensive about Unit 731. The only thing remotely defensive about it was strident tone of the argument with which Ishii justified its existence.

3
Creating Pathology

Rodents and Insects

Rats and fleas, which have spread disease among human beings throughout the ages, were carefully cultivated by the Japanese biological warfare specialists. They harvested rats from Manchuria's rat population, and then enlisted schoolchildren to raise them. It required no difficult technique—just cages, food, and water. Pingfang had rat cultivation cells—they remain today as part of its ruins—which were staffed by Youth Corps members.

On February 26, 1995, the Asahi Broadcasting Company presented a documentary titled "The Mystery of the Rats That Went to the Continent." The camera followed a small group of local high school students in Saitama Prefecture on a project to research stories of farmers in the area who had raised rats during the war years. The students got on their bicycles and went around to different farms asking whether people knew anything about the story of rat farming during the war years. All of the farming families interviewed commented to the effect that "everybody around here was raising rats. It was a source of income." One family even had some of the old, wood-framed rat cages piled up in the shed, each cage built to house six rats. People questioned by the students claimed that they did not know that the rats were being used for spreading disease, although the students were not good enough actors to hide their disbelief. In all fairness to the farmers, however, the project did provide badly needed income, and they would probably have taken any information they received at face value.

In the same area of the prefecture, there had been a center which raised animals for research. This facility was impressed into service as a collection agency for rats, and this fact probably explains why that region became so active in rat farming. The families in the locality brought the animals they had bred to the center, and from there they were transported to Tokyo and the Army Medical College, where they were put upon the return flights to the continent.

It is interesting to note that after the war, the U.S. military kept the families in business. U.S. Army Unit 406 was established in Tokyo to research viruses, and now, in place of the Japanese vehicles, American jeeps became familiar sights in the villages as they came to collect their loads of rats. Perhaps the rate of pay improved with the occupation army.

Producing fleas was slightly trickier. Han Xiao gives an account of flea production in his book *Crimes of Unit 731*. He tells of how in around 1940, the Suzuki Group construction company was putting a new wing on a building at Pingfang, and Chinese laborers from outside were working at one area in the huge compound. A strange rumor circulated among the workers about men who raised fleas. It started soon after the Japanese assembled a group of about ten prisoners all of whom were over fifty years old, and told them to carry their belongings into one of the sheds that served as living quarters.

"Don't worry," the Japanese soldiers reassured them, "you're all over fifty years of age, so there's no need for you to work. Take it easy in here. All you have to do is produce one hundred fleas a day—big ones—and hand them over to us. This is your work."

The prisoners were dressed in heavily padded clothes, and they were given four rules to obey: 1) Do not come into contact with other prisoners; 2) Never talk about this work to anyone; 3) Always sleep with your clothes on; and 4) Do the required work every day.

After about a week, several Japanese dressed in white coveralls began to come every day, and they made the men take off their heavily padded pants and upper wear, turn them inside out, and pick out the fleas that had reached the size of about a match head. These were put into aluminum boxes, and the Japanese took them away. "The smaller fleas are not needed yet," the Japanese advised the men, "but it is prohibited to kill them." The men had to leave the small fleas in the padding until they grew, and in this way some eight hundred to one thousand a day were collected.

The ten men had to go for water themselves and prepare their own meals in their sheds. They were given preventive injections at regular intervals. They were not permitted to remove their clothes or cut their hair even in the hottest weather.

One day, a laborer who came to get water met one of the older men. They checked to see that no one was watching, and the older man told the story of the job he and his fellows were doing. From there, the story of "the ten old men who raise fleas" spread among the laborers.

Without anyone realizing when, the ten men died in succession.

Four Areas of Experimentation

Of the myriad diseases and medical problems into which Unit 731 conducted its research, four areas are particularly prominent. Together, they represent a cross-section of Unit 731's cruelty and perversion, while at the same time providing a glance across the spectrum of the scientific work it conducted.

Cholera

At the human-experiment centers, the first step into researching illness and possible vaccines against it involved getting prisoners sick by injecting them with germs. Once disease had been created in human beings, it would be spread to population centers. After it was ascertained that the disease had taken hold among the locals, the army and its researchers would move in to examine the victims, and test methods of treatment. One method of spreading cholera used domesticated animals as carriers.

Dogs were used to spread cholera in a village about eight kilometers west of Chinan. Dogs caught in the village were fed pork laced with cholera germs, then returned to the village. When the disease finished incubating and became active, the dogs would vomit. Then other dogs would come along and eat the vomit, and they, too, would become infected. The dogs would also be stricken with diarrhea, and the feces would spread the disease among other dogs and to people. Some twenty percent of those who contracted the illness died. Survivors told of hearing the cries of sick people from their homes as they suffered.

Former army captain Kojima Takeo, who was a unit member involved in this cholera campaign, added his own testimony about this strange experiment in an interview: "We were told that we were going out on a cholera campaign, and we were all given inoculations against cholera ten days before starting out. Our objective was to infect all the people in the area. The disease had already developed before we got there, and as we moved into the village everyone scattered. The only ones left were those who were too sick to move. The number of people coming down with the disease kept increasing. Cholera produces a face like a skeleton, vomiting, and diarrhea. And the vomiting and defecating of the people lying sick brought flies swarming around. One after the other, people died."

Captain Kojima's further testimony in the second section of this book offers additional details on this type of operation, as well as other comments on the role of the army in Manchuria.

Epidemic Hemorrhagic Fever (EHF)

The *Asahi* newspaper of April 2, 1943 carried the following story.

ANOTHER VICTORY SHOUT FOR MILITARY MEDICINE

Strange Sickness in Northern Manchuria Conquered

Pathogen for terrible hemorrhagic fever is discovered

The Medical Corps of the invincible Imperial Army raises another victory shout, with a triumph over a strange and unusual disease in northern Manchuria that has been puzzling military and civilian medicine. It has been discovered that the disease is carried by ticks. Not only has the method of transmission of the disease been discovered, but a preventive measure has been established, as well, and development of a treatment seems close at hand.

The pathogen was unknown before this, and the discovery of a new type of carrier that spreads the disease is attracting widespread attention. On the fourth of this month, Tokyo University will hold a convention on parasitology at which [General] Kitano will present his findings. The name for the disease was decided by the army in February of last year. The disease has already been present, however, for many years in northern and eastern Manchuria. It was clearly identified in May 1938 by the Imperial Army. At that time, the disease took the name of the locality where it occurred and other names. The army exerted itself to identify this pathogen for the purposes of disease prevention within the army and to advance sanitation in Manchuria. After the incubation period, a high fever develops, and internal bleeding is present. The death rate is from fifteen to twenty percent.

After Japanese troops moved into Manchuria in the 1930s, there were outbreaks of disease which mystified researchers. It was apparently a local disease which existed around the border area between China and the Soviet Union. Japanese activity in building railroads close to the Soviet border in 1938 had exposed Japanese army personnel to the illness. In 1941, Japanese and Soviet researchers found out almost simultaneously that the agent was a virus; previously, rickettsia bacteria had been suspect. Japanese researchers took advantage of this discovery to earmark the virus as a potential military asset.

After Kitano presented his findings at the convention referred to in the *Asahi* article, he returned to Manchuria and worked on developing the disease into a weapon. In 1944, he published the findings of his research team in various periodicals, including the prestigious *Nihon Byori Gakkaishi (Japan Journal of Pathology)*. In the project, research team members went into areas infested with the disease and collected rats. Ticks which were found on the bodies of the rats were removed, and approximately two hundred of these were ground and mixed into a saline solution. This mixture was then injected, according to the report, into the bodies of monkeys, which were then observed for symptoms of the disease. If the disease manifested in a subject, its blood would be drawn and injected into another subject. The second subject would then be closely observed for development of symptoms. When they appeared, that subject would be dissected, its organs removed, and parts of these ground fine. Then, a saline solution of the organ extract would be injected into another subject, and that subject observed for symptoms. This process was repeated continuously until the pathogen was successfully isolated.

The contents outlined above appeared in an abstract in the medical journal. A medical doctor or researcher reading the manner in which the disease develops, and particularly the fever characteristics, should be able to recognize the subjects not as monkeys but humans. Most obvious is the account of body temperature: the "monkeys" recorded temperatures of up to 40.2 degrees Celsius. Even the sickest monkey's body temperature will never reach that point. Rather, the fever reported was in the range of where it would be for very sick human beings. Moreover, as Professor Tsuneishi points out, the test subjects used in this research were listed simply as "monkeys." Failure to identify the species of an animal in an experiment lowers the value of the paper reporting its results. Where monkeys were actually used, it was common practice to identify the type. Thus, it was an open secret that the simple and unscientific use of the term "monkey" by itself was a code which meant that the subjects were humans.

The medical community knew this. The journal knew this. The readiness with which Kitano publicized this transparent sham—and its acceptance by Japan's medical community at large—is a sad testament to the lack of conflict between the ethical standards of the medical world in Japan and those of Unit 731.

Plague

Armies that want to use disease as a military weapon want something that acts fast and is fatal. Cholera, for instance, with its incubation period of about twenty days, would not generally be a feasible tactical weapon. (This helps explain the emphasis on vaccine research in the case of that disease; Unit 731's work with cholera would appear aimed more at preventing it among Japanese troops than making active use of it on the battlefield.) Plague, on the other hand, starts killing within three days, and has a long, illustrious history as a weapon of biological warfare. One of the earliest recorded uses of plague in warfare was in 1346 in the Crimea, where the Genoese army was besieged inside a walled fortress by the Mongols. When plague broke out among the latter, they turned this development to their advantage by throwing the dead, diseased bodies over the Genoese ramparts. After that, the Mongols unwittingly carried the plague through Asia, and the troops from Genoa carried it back to Europe, where it became the feared "Black Death."

With its proven credentials as a terrible and effective instrument of war, plague was one of the first diseases focused in on by the Ishii unit researchers. They apparently placed a lot of weight on researching—and causing—this disease, and as many as six plague attacks were reportedly carried out. The best known of these operations are outlined here.

In October 1940 a plague attack was conducted against the Kaimingjie area of the port city of Ningbo. This was a joint operation by Unit 731 and one of its affiliates, Nanjing-based Unit 1644. In this operation, plague germs mixed with wheat, corn, cloth scraps, and cotton were dropped from the air.

Qian Guifa, a resident of the area attacked, was fourteen years old at the time and working in a tofu shop. He was infected, but managed to recover, and it is said that he is the only living person today who can bear witness to the Japanese biological warfare experiment at Ningbo. His testimony has been recorded in video documentary and in printed literature in Japan. He recounts: "One day, a Japanese plane flew over and kept circling. Then, it dropped something that looked like smoke. It was wheat flour and corn and other things. The next day people started getting sick. Three days later, the tofu shop owner's two children were dead, and other people were getting sick and dying. Nobody could understand what had happened. My own family died, one after the other. There was misery all around.

"Everyone who died did so in pain and agony, going into convulsions. At first the bodies turned red, then after death they turned black."

More than one hundred persons died within a few days after the attack. The affected area was closed to the public and remained sealed off until the 1960s, when it was ascertained positively that there was no further risk of infection.

Government records still existing in China show the results of the plague attacks and the deaths which followed. A Chinese specialist on disease prevention and plague tells how he kept the disease from spreading to other areas.

"On the twenty-ninth, three days after the Japanese plane came, I entered the Ningbo area that had been attacked. The first thing I did was separate the people seriously affected, those lightly affected, and the healthy ones. Then, I encircled the infected area of the attack zone with a wall about a meter deep and a meter and a half high, so that rats could not escape. Six hundred people were moved south. When November came, we burned everything in the enclosed area, and in this way we stopped the plague from spreading. According to my records, ninety-seven people died."

Then, in September 1942, another attack was carried out by the two units, with Ishii himself commanding the operation. A survivor reports:

> I was fifteen years old at the time, and I remember everything clearly. The Japanese plane spread something that looked like smoke. A few days later we found dead rats all over the village. At the same time, people came down with high fevers and aches in the lymph nodes. Every day, people died. Crying could be heard all through the village.
>
> My mother and father—in all, eight people in my family—died. I was the only one in my family left.

My mother had a high fever all day. She was crying for water, and clawing at her throat. Then, she let out a roar like a lion, and died before my eyes. Altogether, three hundred eighty people in the village died. At times, as many as twenty people died in one day.

As soon as the first people started dying, Japanese came into the village wearing protective clothing and masks. The went around the village for three days, giving injections to the people. They administered two shots, one to the arm and one to the chest. Some of the people who got these shots also died.

The Japanese researchers took over a house on top of a hill about a kilometer away from the attack area to use as a vivisection laboratory. Another plague attack survivor, Qian Tangjiang, gave his account of the biological warfare experiment: "We were told that if we went to Rin's house at the top of the hill, we would get treated. My friend told me that his wife went to the house for treatment, and later was seen strapped to a table with her body split open. Her feet were still moving; there's no doubt that she was dissected alive."

A woman of the village, Wang Julian, also discussed the plague attack: "Five members of my family died. My mother and father both suffered from swollen lymph nodes, then a high fever. They died in agony. I was taken to Rin's house, also, and I was there for two days. Then, the next day, the Japanese went into the village again, and I ran away. The villagers gave me herbal medicines, and in time my fever went down and I lived through it."

These successful air attacks showed that disease could be delivered by air, and so the army doctors redoubled their efforts to produce and accumulate rats and fleas. Still, imperfections remained in the system. The early attacks had all been carried out by slow, low-flying planes that were effective against peaceful, unarmed villages or cities. Battlefield conditions would be far more demanding. Ishii wanted to have the ability to deliver pathogens from higher altitudes, and started developing a series of bombs that could deliver rodents and insects from greater heights.

The test ground at Anda started seeing drops from higher altitudes using different prototypes of biological warfare bombs. Early attempts had proven that explosives were not practical for releasing the bombs' contents since the detonations killed the insects. Glass bombs were experimented with, and then Ishii remembered Japan's ceramic heritage. He went into villages where traditional kilns had turned out ceramic wares, and ordered bombs made to his specifications.

It was not the first use of ceramics for war. The secret poison gas factory at Okunoshima had ordered ceramic gas bombs from the centuries-old pottery makers in the Kyoto region. Japan had also made ceramic land mines, avoiding use of precious metals in anticipation of a possible Allied invasion of the home islands. Only the sensors on top were metal.

The artisans making Ishii's bombs reportedly had no idea what they were making. Their orders were to follow the plans and produce the "objects" he designed. About sixty-five centimeters in length, each had a screw-top in the nose that could be removed so that pathogens could be loaded in.

New light on the pathogenic air attacks on the Chinese population centers was shed by Okijima, the former Unit

731 member who, at seventy-eight years of age, broke a half-century of silence and gave his observations on the civilian makeup of Unit 731. In 1939, Okijima became a civilian employee of the army and was sent to Unit 731. He was assigned to work with bacteria in the laboratory of the unit's air wing. On the morning of the attack on Ningbo, Okijima dressed in an anti-contamination protective suit, and pumped liquid pathogens from oil drums into two tanks fixed to the belly of the plane that would be used in the attack. The combination of this liquid and the wheat flour described by the resident of Ningbo might account for the smoky appearance of the plane's payload.

Okijima also explained one of several preliminary tests that was conducted beforehand.

> We used the airfield inside the Unit 731 complex. A truck filled with eggs drove into the airport. Several hundred eggs were broken into a drum and mixed, then loaded onto a plane. The meteorological team was checking wind direction and velocity. We placed square boards, fifty centimeters to a side, on the ground at regular intervals and had the eggs sprayed from the air. Then, we studied the boards to see what kind of dispersal and coverage we got.
>
> Once we used the inside of a huge mausoleum-type structure and a stopwatch to measure the rate of fall of rice husks in a windless environment. We poured dyes into the Songhua [Sungari] River to see how far they travel and what concentrations remain at various distances from the source. This was to determine the effectiveness of an attack by pathogens added to rivers.

Liquid would have done away with the problem of handling living animals, such as the insects and rats discussed earlier, in battle conditions. Other factors, however, apparently prevented its proving a suitable vehicle. Okijima said that the Ningbo attack was the only time he handled liquid pathogens.

Frostbite

Professor Tsuneishi has conducted nearly two decades of research into the activities of Unit 731, and his knowledge of its history and activities is encyclopedic. Of everything that went on in the prison cells, on the dissection tables, and in the research labs, he has expressed his opinion that the cruelest experiments of all were those which concerned frostbite research.

These tests were directed by Dr. Yoshimura Hisato, a physiologist from the same school, Kyoto Imperial University, as Ishii. According to Yoshimura's memoirs, Ishii came to recruit him for the experiments in Manchuria, and Yoshimura asked what a physiologist could do in a bacteriological research unit. He said he could understand his being used in submarine research, for example, or in high-altitude research for pilots. But what, he asked, could he do for the Ishii unit?

Japanese military leaders were always looking at the possibility of having to fight the Soviets. In 1905, after sacrifices and feats called superhuman by foreign observers, Japan had crushed Russia's sea and land forces and established herself solidly in Manchuria. Since then, Russo-Japanese relations had remained icy, and Moscow remained on Tokyo's list of potential adversaries. Now, Japan's incursion into China was again putting her eyeball-to-eyeball with Moscow. If another clash came, it was sure to be in cold weather.

In fact, cold-weather combat had already established itself as a problem. At the time of the Manchurian Incident that began Japan's occupation of parts of China in 1931, army medics treated large numbers of Japanese soldiers who suffered from frostbite. Usually, fingers and toes would be affected. Frostbitten and normal parts of limbs were marked with blue or green dividing lines. Treatment of the problem normally involved application of ointment to affected areas and amputating where necessary (without anesthetic). This experience made it clearer than ever that cold-weather fighting demanded prior knowledge of frostbite prevention and treatment.

Training for the Russo-Japanese War had included winter maneuvers by Japanese troops in the mountains of northern Japan. Preparation for the next round of potential winter warfare would be supervised by physiologist Yoshimura. Yoshimura was called to Manchuria to conduct cold-weather tests on human subjects, and one of the standard methods that he employed in his research was deliberate induction of frostbite.

A member of the Yoshimura team, Nishi Toshihide, was captured by the Soviets, and he testified at the Khabarovsk trials as to how some of the experiments were carried out. He also stated that 16-mm movies had been made as a visual record of the experiments. Reports from other Unit 731 members corroborate his statements.

People were taken from prison into below-freezing temperatures. They were tied up, with their arms bared and soaked with water. Water was poured over the arms regularly; sometimes the ice that formed on them would be chipped away and water again poured over. The researcher would strike the limbs regularly with a club. When an arm made a sound like a wooden board's being hit, this indicated that the limb was frozen through, and from there different methods of treatments were tested. Legs and feet were exposed to similar treatment.

Temperatures in Manchuria can reach as low as minus twenty to thirty degrees Celsius. Some of the tests were conducted outdoors in these winter conditions. At times, electric fans were used to speed the freezing. At Pingfang, Yoshimura had his own large refrigerator lab that allowed him to freeze subjects all year round and reach even lower temperatures than out in the open— temperatures that reached as low as minus seventy degrees Celsius.

Some experiments resulted in the flesh and muscle falling from the bones. Others left the bones so brittle that they were shattered by the blows from the clubs. Either way, the eventual result was the same: gangrene and the rotting away of extremities. Several former Unit 731 members have commented on seeing victims of the experiments. They reported that the victims "had no hands . . . no feet."

A miniature model of a frostbite experiment was displayed at the Unit 731 exhibitions: It depicts an experiment being performed on a Russian prisoner. Chinese were also used as fodder for the freezing experiments, and some of the victims were women. Yoshimura conducted his frostbite experiments right up until the end of the war. One of the discoveries for which Yoshimura subsequently became famous was that the previously standard treatment of rubbing frozen limbs until they thawed was not the most efficient way of restoring them. Through trial and error, he showed that the best treatment was placing the affected parts in warm water between thirty-seven degrees (normal human body temperature) and forty degrees Celsius. There is no way to count the number of people and human limbs he consumed in arriving at this finding.

After the war, Yoshimura became an eminent authority on polar human biology. He held university posts and later became president of the Kyoto Prefectural University of Medicine. Newspaper articles later came out accusing him of conducting human experimentation, but he denied the accusations. Then, in 1982, a Japanese newspaper carried an article on a paper which Yoshimura presented at a meeting of the Japan Physiology Society. Interestingly, the article identified him only as "A." However, the article's mention of his age, a description of the school of which he was president, the fact of his residence in Kyoto, and other clues made "A's" identity quite clear.

The article was headlined "Human Experimentation Blatantly Presented in Lecture." It announced that "a former member of Unit 731 presented the results of his human experimentation on frostbite in Manchuria at a meeting of the Japan Physiology Society. The results of his wartime research were printed in the society's journal, and the medical community directed heavy criticism against the group and its behavior.

"Last year, at the fifty-eighth meeting of the Japan Physiology Society in the city of Tokushima, this member presented a lecture on the 'History of My Research.' His talk included a description of ethnic comparisons of adaptability to cold."

Yoshimura was reported as commenting with pride that "the English-language *Japan Journal of Physiology* carried the report completed by me and my late assistant in three issues between August 1950 and February 1952." The printed report covered tests on more than five hundred males from the ages of eight through forty-eight. Test subjects included Mongols, Chinese, Siberian tribesmen, and others. The tests were conducted by placing coils on the subjects' fingers and immersing them in ice water. Changes were measured in skin surface, and data analyzed according to age and ethnic stock to determine a correlation between cold resistance and race.

This experiment does not seem especially cruel, and Yoshimura has criticized the press on numerous occasions for exaggerating the callousness of his research. What has not been brought to public view, however, are the frostbite tests which destroyed the limbs and then the lives of their subjects. Eyewitness testimonies about having seen such tests and their victims with blackened extremities provide evidence that he was engaged in destructive work.

The journal of the Japan Physiology Society was even criticized by its own members for publishing Yoshimura's report without censuring his methods. Former students of Yoshimura have commented on his attitude at class lectures, about how very cavalier he was about using and discarding human beings for research. Students were constantly amazed that he never seemed to consider anything he did to be wrong, and associates frequently advised him to be more prudent about describing his methods. Apparently, he never saw a need to heed their advice.

In celebration of his seventy-seventh birthday, considered auspicious by Japanese, Yoshimura Hisato wrote a book of his reminiscences which was published in 1984. In its pages, he mentions his association with Unit 731 several times, yet defends himself against accusations that his experiments were cruel. He shows one photograph of a young Chinese in a laboratory undergoing an apparently painless test, with hands placed in cold water to record heat loss. "This person is obviously undergoing very little stress," he comments. His other tests get no mention.

Yoshimura's human experimentation led to his removal from the chairmanship of an academic organization in Japan. Student protests about issues including his human experimentation also led to his stepping down from the presidency of Kyoto Prefectural University of Medicine.

In 1981, reporters from the *Mainichi* newspaper searched out former members of Unit 731 for interviews. (Three of these appear in Part 2 of this book.) They approached a "former army technician who became president of a public medical university after the war" and asked him about human experimentation. His answer, given in his office at the Kyoto Prefectural University of Medicine, was simultaneously evasive and unabashed: "Human experimentation? Maybe my subordinates did that, but I never did. But you people are thinking wrong. Even that did happen, it was war. The orders came from the country. All the responsibility lies with the country. The individual is not responsible."

Yoshimura's special, two-story tall "refrigerator laboratory" still stands at the Pingfang ruins.

4
End and Aftermath

Attempted Biological Warfare Against the Americans

Only six months after Pearl Harbor, the battle of Midway in June 1942 marked the end of Japan's string of victories in the Pacific. From that point on, the territory under her control continued to ebb away. As the situation grew darker, Tokyo began considering measures as desperate as the position in which it found itself. Ishii looked to biological warfare, which had had devastating effect against the Chinese, as a weapon that could help Japan make a comeback against Allied forces.

In 1944, the United States attacked Saipan, an island in the western Pacific. For the Japanese, it was vital that the island remain out of American hands, for it would make a perfect staging ground for large-scale bombing raids against Japan itself. Ishii dispatched a special team of about twenty men equipped with biological weapons, under the command of two army medical officers from his alma mater of Kyoto Imperial University, to launch an attack of plague and perhaps other diseases against the enemy. Their ship was sunk en route, however, and the pathogens never reached the battlefield.

As 1945 arrived, the Japanese waited for an American landing on Okinawa. Not all the defense preparations were taking place near the prospective battlefield, however; in far-off China, the Ishii organization was making plans to meet the invaders with plague bacteria. Ironically, Okinawans themselves never heard anything about these plans until January 1994, when the Unit 731 Exhibition opened there.

While the touring exhibition spread shock among Japanese wherever it opened, it hit home especially hard and deep for Okinawans. Fifty years after they were educated to sacrifice every man, woman, and child to repel the invaders, in a place where civilians armed with bamboo spears and indoctrinated into dying for the emperor charged into guns, news of yet another Japanese betrayal broke. A seventy-one-year-old former member of Unit 1855 in Beijing gave testimony that appeared in the (Japanese-language) *Okinawa Times*.

Ito Kageaki, now living in Yokohama, was assigned to the Beijing unit toward the end of 1943. His work there entailed raising fleas for spreading plague. He told of the education he and his comrades received at the unit, and how an officer advised them that "this kind of tactic was not permitted until now, but if we employ it, it will be against the American landing at Okinawa."

Ito recalled how his detachment had first consisted of only five or six men. Then, from around 1944, personnel and facilities were expanded. "Plague germs were brought in from other units," he recounted, "and Chinese prisoners were experimented upon." Ito himself was never required to carry out human experimentation, but as a member of the unit he was a witness to it.

After the war, Ito never spoke to his parents or family about his experiences in the unit. He worked for the

Japanese National Railways, and was afraid of losing his job if he brought up the subject. Then, in 1988, he made a trip to China, met with citizens there, and gained a completely different perspective.

"There was no reason for Japan to make China an enemy," he commented, "and I should not carry my experiences to the grave. I want our past to be an education for the next generation."

After returning to Japan from his China trip, he started telling his story. The Unit 731 Exhibition's arrival in Okinawa gave him an opportunity to tell Okinawans of the real position they occupied in the minds of the Japanese military: "Tokyo was under air attack, Japanese were making suicide stands in the Pacific, and there were other setbacks for Japan. The situation grew progressively worse. Okinawa could be thrown away if Japan could gain some military advantage." He added, "I question whether the military would have planned for BW [biological warfare] if the landing had been projected for Kyushu instead of Okinawa. I believe that behind the military's thinking was the fact that this is the former Kingdom of the Ryukyus [as distinct from Japan proper], and this shows the racial disdain the Japanese military had for the Okinawans."

One of the local organizing committee members for Okinawa's Unit 731 exhibition, a high school teacher, gave his impression of Ito's recollections: "If this is true, it sends a shiver down the spine. This makes the sacrifices in the Okinawa battle even more pitiful."

In the end, the attack never came together in time for execution. A merciful coincidence of timing thus spared the people of Japan's southernmost prefecture from further suffering at the hands of their Imperial Japanese Army "protectors."

Even this was not the most shocking idea conceived by Japan's military planners, however. Recent evidence points to a plan to carry Japan's biological warfare program to the United States itself.

The top navy leaders who looked to biological warfare as a last-ditch effort to turn the tide of the war set their sights no lower than the American mainland itself. They targeted it for an attack that would combine elements of previous attacks on Chinese cities and villages with a *kamikaze* delivery system. A former officer of the Imperial Japanese Navy who had been involved with the plan let the world hear about it for the first time in an interview carried by the *Sankei* newspaper on August 14, 1977. Former captain Eno Yoshio, seventy-three years old and living in Hiroshima at the time he talked to the paper, was closely involved in the operation from the beginning. The *Sankei* article quoted Eno as admitting that "this is the first time I have said anything about Operation PX, because it involved the rules of war and international law. The plan was not put into actual operation, but I felt that just the fact that it was formulated would cause international misunderstanding. I never even leaked anything to the staff of the war history archives at the Japan Defense Agency, and I don't feel comfortable talking about it even now. But, at the time, Japan was losing badly, and any means to win would have been all right."

The Japanese navy had submarines nicknamed "underwater aircraft carriers," which could generally hold from one to three seaplanes inside watertight compartments at deck height under their conning towers. When the subs surfaced, the hangar compartments opened into launch catapults. When the planes landed, they came alongside their mother ships, and they were hoisted back aboard with winches. The I-400 submarine, the only ship of its class, was a large sub capable of carrying three planes. This boat was earmarked for the attack on America's west coast.

The sub had a displacement of 3,530 tons, an underwater speed of six and a half knots, and a surface speed of eighteen knots. It was diesel-powered and snorkel-equipped, so that its combustion engines could run even while the boat was submerged. This characteristic enabled it to use one of its two engines for propulsion, while it charged its batteries with the other. At sixteen knots on the surface, it had a normal range of thirty-one thousand nautical miles. Its range could be extended by filling the ballast tanks with fuel oil instead of water. Filling the ballast tanks would, of course, mean that the sub could not surface until after a sufficient amount of fuel had been consumed, but Allied air and naval presence in the Pacific in the early part of 1945 would make submerged travel prudent at any rate. Reaching the American mainland seemed to be no problem, at least as far as technology was concerned.

All discussion of the ultra-secret plan, first proposed toward the end of December 1944, was confined to a special tactical room set aside at the headquarters of the Naval General Staff in Hibiya, Tokyo. There were two main drawbacks to conducting this operation as a purely naval venture. One was a lack of data regarding the intended pathogens. The other was a lack of the pathogens themselves. For this, the nation's highest authority on biological warfare was called in, and Ishii became special advisor to the top army man in the project, Colonel Hattori Takushiro. One might imagine Ishii's anticipation as he envisioned American high-density population centers filled with agony, with citizens turning to blackened corpses. It would be a larger-scale success of—

indeed a capstone to—his attacks on Chinese cities and villages.

The plan was initiated as a joint army-navy project under the code name "Operation PX." It called for the sub to approach the American shore, then launch its planes and spread plague, cholera, and perhaps other pathogens from the air. The submarine crews would run ashore carrying germs. The entire attack was planned as a suicide mission.

The project moved forward from a foundation of biological warfare intelligence provided by Ishii and Unit 731, and the plan was finalized on March 26, 1945. Then, at the last moment, General Umezu Yoshijiro, Chief of the General Staff, stepped in and ordered the plan scrapped. He reasoned that "if bacteriological warfare is conducted, it will grow from the dimension of war between Japan and America to an endless battle of humanity against bacteria. Japan will earn the derision of the world."

The officers working on the attack plan objected fiercely, but Umezu's decision prevailed. There is little doubt that an American city would have been another Ningbo on a larger scale.

Interestingly, about two weeks before the finalization of the plan, America brought a new weapon into the war with an incendiary attack on a large, lower-class neighborhood of Tokyo. Even among the almost continuous air raids over Japan, the Great Tokyo Air Raid had been the most devastating so far, with an estimated one hundred thousand civilians burned to death by a combination of conventional incendiaries and America's new contribution to modern weaponry, napalm. Even this failed to deter Umezu from his veto of a germ attack on America.

General Umezu was later given the inglorious duty of representing Japan's army in signing the instrument of capitulation aboard the U.S.S. Missouri. At first he refused, then agreed to go only if it were considered a direct order from the emperor. Umezu was later tried for and found guilty of war crimes at the Tokyo War Crimes Trials. His single-handed prevention of the bacteriological attack on America never surfaced there.

In August 1947, the Chief of Naval Intelligence in Washington released a top-secret, hundred-page-long document entitled "Naval Aspects of Biological Warfare." It was produced in cooperation with the Biological Warfare Section of the Intelligence Division of the War Department General Staff to "present as accurate a picture as possible" of the material it covered. It discussed biological warfare research in major countries such as the United States, Great Britain, Germany, Italy, the Soviet Union, and Japan. The report asserted: "It is doubtful if humanitarian principles have ever been responsible for failure to employ man-made epidemics."

Ironically, the Naval Intelligence report came out about halfway through the Tokyo trials, where Umezu was sentenced to life in jail. The secret died with him at Sugamo Prison in 1949.

Covering the Traces

As the end of the war loomed, Japan came to expect a Soviet thrust into Manchuria, and the facilities of Unit 731 and its branch units were blown up to destroy evidence of their existence and the horrors they had perpetrated. At Zhongma, the construction was so superb that its destruction was difficult. Calling it a "fortress" was no exaggeration; while the installation was built for the purpose of research and development, it obviously had the structural strength to withstand attack.

Pingfang, the center at Dalian, and other units were destroyed, but other facilities remain standing to this day. The staunch building in Nanjing that served as home to Unit 1644, sometimes called the Tama Unit, is now used is a hospital. People can visit the rooms on the second floor where rats and fleas were once raised. They can visit the third floor, where infected *maruta* were dissected, admission was permitted only to authorized persons wearing protective clothing and masks, and disinfection at the doorway was required. They can visit the fourth floor, which was a prison.

Skeleton crews stayed behind in China to carry out the destruction, while the major part of the staff and their families, feeling the Soviets' breath upon their necks, cleared out. The South Manchuria Railway was efficient to the end. A special train carried unit members from Harbin and Pingfang, then traveled south, through the Korean peninsula. After crossing to Japan by sea, they took another special train north through Kanazawa, where some members reportedly used the Noma Shrine for a hideout. The special train continued on to Niigata Prefecture, at which point the members split up and used regular public transportation.

In Manchuria, Ishii boarded the train for one leg of the journey, during which he set forth his rules that members were not to take jobs in public offices, were not to contact each other from then on, and were to "take this secret to the grave." He took films and records with him, and returned to Japan by plane.

At Pingfang today, remnants of the fortress still remain, preserved as a monument to human inhumanity. The massive double stacks of the boiler room stand like a morbid tombstone, and seem to hang on to existence just as thousands of captives there must have hung on until the end, hoping that something, somehow would save them—or part of them—from destruction. The Ping-fang fortress of the medical inquisition is clinging to life, keeping the memory of screams, cries, and death agonies from disappearing completely.

American Occupation

As the end of the war brought Allied forces and civilian personnel to Japan by air and sea, a new chapter was about to begin for Unit 731. The postwar story of the outfit begins in September 1945, with the docking of the American ship Sturgess in Yokohama. Among those on board was Lieutenant Colonel Murray Sanders. A highly regarded microbiologist who had been a lecturer at Columbia University, Sanders had entered the military and been attached to Camp Detrick (later Fort Detrick) in Maryland, the American military's center for biological weapons research and development. The work done there would have been at the heart of retaliation which President Franklin Delano Roosevelt had threatened for what he termed Japan's "inhumane form of warfare" in China through biological weaponry.

As the Sturgess worked its way toward the western part of Tokyo Bay and the port of Yokohama, Naito Ryoichi waited on the pier. Naito, one of the men closest to Ishii, and the number-two man in Ishii's research laboratory in Tokyo, already had a history of duplicitous dealing with foreigners. Before the war, he had studied in Germany and in the U.S., at the University of Pennsylvania. During his stay in America, he had walked into the Rockefeller Institute in New York with a letter of introduction from the Japanese embassy in Washington and a request for samples of yellow fever virus. His reason for the request, he had explained to the people at the institute, was that upon his return to Japan, he would be working for the Japanese army in Manchuria in developing a vaccine for the disease. When the Americans refused, perhaps because of mounting U.S.-Japanese tensions over the latter country's aggression in China, he attempted to resort to bribery. In the end, he came back to Japan without the yellow fever viruses.

Back in Japan, Naito wrote up secret reports on ways of increasing the virulence of pathogens, methods of bacteriological warfare, and other subjects that were being handled in the Ishii organization.

As the crew of the Sturgess threw the ship's berthing lines onto the dock, Naito purposefully awaited it, ready to play his role in launching Unit 731 into its postwar odyssey. Japan's information network had found out that Sanders would be on board, and that he would be in charge of investigating Japan's biological warfare activities. Years later, Sanders himself described the scene this way in an interview: "My mission was biological warfare. I was to find what the Japanese had done, and when the Sturgess docked in Yokohama, there was Dr. Naito. He came straight toward me. He seemed to have had a photograph of me, and said that he was my interpreter."

"Did you know at that time," Sanders was asked, "that he was a member of Unit 731?"

"I didn't even know what 731 was."

Sanders installed himself in his office and started his job of meeting with Japanese believed to be concerned with research into and/or actual employment of biological warfare. And from there, with the dust of World War II still hanging over Tokyo, a new contest started. Rather than making offensive war against its enemies, Unit 731 now went on the defensive against the occupation forces. The data gained from human experimentation once again became ammunition: this time in the bargaining room, rather than on the battlefield. The Japanese hoped to use their knowledge as a tool for gaining freedom from prosecution as war criminals.

Sanders offered other memories of Naito, too: "He was a very humble, shy person . . . very careful. He went home every night and came back the next morning. If you're interested, I found out later that he didn't go home, but went to the various Japanese headquarters." At those offices, Naito conferred with others on what information should be given to Sanders, and what should be withheld. Naito also kept the Japanese officials apprised of the content and progress of his discussions with Sanders. Naito's purpose was to get between Sanders and anyone connected with Unit 731 with whom Sanders came into contact. For this reason, the American failed to make any considerable amount of progress. Naito, the interpreter-cum-information filter, was sometimes evasive, sometimes contradictory in this game of cat-and-mouse.

At last, Sanders was up against a wall and told Naito that if things continued the way they were going, the Communists would be coming into the picture. "I said that," Sanders recounts in the interview, "because the Japanese exhibited a deadly fear of the Communists, and they didn't want them messing around. He appeared the next morning with a manuscript which contained startling material. It was fundamentally dynamite. The manuscript said, in essence, that the Japanese were involved in biological warfare." The document, Sanders stated, gave the line of command of the Japanese military, with all the departments "implicated, plus or minus." Obviously, as much as America wanted the information, the Japanese had an equal interest in avoiding the "justice" of the Soviet legal system, at whose hands their fate would be easy enough to predict. His gambit appeared to have succeeded.

Sanders took the document to General Douglas MacArthur, the Supreme Commander for the Allied Powers (SCAP), and from there the balance of options was weighed. There was information that America wanted, and on an exclusive basis. That would mean America's turning its back on the forthcoming war crimes trials and striking a deal, independently of the judiciary proceedings, with the men who had the data. Sanders recalls MacArthur as having said, "Well, if you feel that you cannot draw out the information, we are not given to torture." So, deprived of the stick of physical duress, the American microbiologist went back to Naito with a carrot instead. MacArthur would assure Naito that in exchange for the information, the informants would not be brought to trial. "This made a deep impression, and the data came in waves after that . . . we could hardly keep up with it."

In December 1994, a written record of several meetings that took place between Sanders and top-echelon Japanese officers surfaced in the home of an eighty-four-year-old Japanese former staff officer. It was published in the Spring 1995 issue of the Japanese quarterly magazine *Senso Sekinin Kenkyu (The Report on Japan's War Responsibility)*, with the agreement that the owner's identity remain confidential. The record was written in Japanese by the Japanese interpreter at the meetings, and excerpts appeared in the article. The meetings took place at MacArthur's headquarters in the Dai-Ichi Sogo Building on

October 9, 11, and 16, 1946. The interpreter for the first
two meetings is listed as Kamei Kan'ichiro, "a member
of the House of Representatives with very strong ties to
unit leader Ishii." (Kamei's continuing involvement with
postwar Unit 731 members and their bargaining efforts
belies claims over the years that the government was in
the dark about Ishii's activities.) Questioning proceeded
along the lines of how and why the unit was formed,
development of different types of biological warfare bombs
and outdoor tests of these, what happened at the time of
the Soviet invasion of Manchuria, the system of cultur-
ing bacteria using incubators, production of vaccine, and
other germane issues.

The article in the journal simply lists the names of the
participants in the exchange as "S," "M," and "N." The
first two letters are explained explicitly as referring re-
spectively to Sanders and a Colonel Masuda Tomosada,
who had served with Unit 731 in Manchuria from 1945.
"N" is left unexplained, but could only be Naito since he,
with his English ability, had been maneuvering questioning all throughout the postwar investigations and had
attended many of the sessions with Sanders (whether
wanted or not). The term "BK" in the Japanese notes is
deduced by the author of the article to mean development of biological weapons. This is an excerpt from the
notes of the meeting of October 9, 1945:

> N: I brought Colonel Masuda with me, the man
> we spoke of the other day . . .
> S: Did you not engage in BK research?
> M: Yes, I did.
> S: I would like you to tell me about that biological
> warfare research.
> M: I know about BK and will gladly talk about it,

but first I want to mention that what I am about to say is my own opinion. I believe that you will not use it for political reasons.

I know that you [Sanders] spoke yesterday with Lieutenant Colonel "N", and I feel secure in speaking freely about this now.

The transcript of this meeting notes that "the 'statement' made to Lieutenant Colonel Naito in this investigation is data for a secret report to the [American] president. It is not to be revealed. Rather, if a problem concerning BK arises among the various countries, America's knowing our situation can dispose of the problem to Japan's advantage. This is not concerned with the question of searching out war criminals." This shows that the proposal—made with the involvement of the American president—to grant immunity from war crimes was already on the table less than two months after the war's end.

While Naito was capable of using and disposing of human beings with no more compassion than scientists extend to lab rats, superficially he appeared to have much in common with Sanders. Both men, after all, were researchers, not military men, and yet both had ended up soldiers and even attained the same rank of lieutenant colonel. Thus, the main players in the crucial first encounter between American authorities and Unit 731 seem to have interacted not on the basis of victor and vanquished, but more like peers: Sanders the scholar looking through his colleague Naito's microscope. Naito, a mild-mannered man described as "friendly" even by a Singaporean who had worked for him cultivating rats, was also crafty enough to play ping-pong with the information Sanders wanted, so that Sanders' first reports on his investigations advised his superiors that biological warfare in the Japanese army had been an "unimportant minor activity." He covered himself though, by expressing doubt that all had been revealed.

Shortly after the initial doors of information had been pried open by Sanders' threat of the Communists' participation in the investigations, and knowing that MacArthur had promised immunity to former members of Unit 731, Ishii felt sufficiently protected to come out from hiding. Then, while the Allies were tied up with the burden of preparing for the upcoming war crimes tribunal, Ishii was placed under house arrest. There, he was made available for questioning by the successor to Murray Sanders, Lieutenant Colonel Arvo Thompson.

Sent by Camp Detrick to continue the investigation into biological warfare activities, Thompson was not as soft as Sanders, not so easy to brush off with evasive answers. Thompson reached closer to the scope of the experiments but the magnificence of Ishii's organizational skills and the scale of the unit's operations eluded him, as well. He concluded that civilian scientists and research facilities were not involved.

One thing the Japanese have demonstrated throughout history is their ability to form complex—at times, frustratingly byzantine—organizations to coordinate complicated activities. Feudal Japan in the seventeenth through nineteenth centuries was made up of some two hundred fifty feudal domains (the number fluctuating as new ones were created, others abolished) with a complex and clearly defined bureaucracy at the center. No European country had such a precision-cut hierarchy of interknit functions and responsibilities. The shogunate also organized what is considered the world's first secret police as an arm of government, as well as an espionage network. The fact that Japan had a fully developed money economy by the early seventeenth century—even to the point of using a variety of paper credits in major business transactions—is another indication of an advanced sense of organization.

Ishii's empire was, in a sense, a mirror image of the feudal webwork, even down to the police network. Lingering Confucian relationships between established researchers and their disciples meant that medical students were under the control of their instructors. Data from the prison/research cells circulating back through Tokyo and out to the nation's medical research facilities tied the military and civilian medical worlds together in a complicated, logical framework. The development of biological weapons was, in fact, sometimes a cover for ordinary medical research using extraordinary methods available to the Japanese only in the Ishii organization. This was one aspect of the machinery which eluded the Americans. The net was broad and deep, yet to the Americans, still invisible.

Thompson left Japan without getting too much closer to reality. Back at Camp Detrick, his findings were evaluated but led to no firm conclusions.

Superpower Jockeying

Meanwhile, in the first week of May 1946, about four months after Ishii was first interviewed, the International Military Tribunal for the Far East convened. From initial appearances, it should have made sense for the Americans to want to question members of Unit 731. Indications of biological warfare activities by the Japanese had trickled into Allied hands even well before the end of the war. Also, Japanese POWs, many of whom had backgrounds in military hygiene and related fields, served as a significant source of accounts. Reports of Japanese biological warfare activities in China had even prompted a warning from the American president as early as 1943 that if they were not halted, the U.S. would retaliate "in full measure."

Among other examples of American wartime discoveries of Japan's bacteriological warfare is an official U.S. research report titled "Japanese Violations of the Laws of War," dated June 1945. It catalogues some evidence of Japanese biological warfare, and it is certain that it reached the highest levels of the American government: one copy of the report was labeled "Personal copy for General of the Army Douglas MacArthur." It carries the statement of a prisoner captured on May 12, 1944. His family name of Rin would be Chinese, not Japanese, but he was listed as a Japanese POW of the Americans. He stated that he had been a civilian employee working in the Bacteriology Department of Chuzan University at Guangzhou, and was quoted in the report as saying that in June 1941, "he heard that Major General Ishii, Shiro was conducting experiments with bacillus bombs at branch of Army Medical College in Harbin, Manchuria. Previously, Major General Ishii had been head of Laboratory Section, Army Medical College at Tokyo."

Other damning entries appear in the report, as well. One is an "extract from loose handwritten sheets containing fragmentary notes on various types of bombs. Undated and unclassified, owner and unit not stated, captured Philippine Islands, December 1944: MK-7 bacterial bomb (BYORYOKIN) 1 kilogram." Another item in the book shows a list of Japanese possessions falling into American hands. One such item is a printed manual of "Field Service and Supply" dated August 1941, and with "many pages missing." A section of this document is listed in the U.S. report as titled "Subject Matter— Bombing, Gas and Bacteria (these pages torn out.)"

The end of the war did not mean an end to such reports. If anything, the volume of information arriving at SCAP headquarters exceeded that available during wartime, flowing in almost from the time of the beginning of the Occupation. Moreover, Joseph B. Keenan, chief of the International Prosecution Section (IPS), had received reports of biological warfare activities. Nonetheless, no action had yet been taken to investigate whether any of the participants in Japan's biological warfare activities should be called up before the tribunal.

Moscow seemed to have stronger feelings on the issue than its ostensible ally Washington. With the trials underway, the prosecutor for the U.S.S.R. made a request to interview Ishii and two other leading researchers, Colonels Kikuchi and Ota, in connection with biological warfare experiments. Information from Japanese POWs captured by the Soviets in Manchuria had suggested to them a need to investigate Japan's biological warfare program further. The information that the POWs had supplied to the Soviets concerned experiments by these men using Chinese and Manchurians. The Soviets were assuming—or claiming to assume—that supplementary war crimes trials would be authorized by the United States. And, of course, they wanted to see all information relevant to Unit 731.

The Soviets were interested in Ishii and his organization for three important reasons. One was the proximity of the unit's operations to Soviet territory. Next, of course, was the desire for revenge for Japan's use of biological warfare against Soviet soldiers. The third motivation was the prospect of obtaining grist for the propaganda mill.

Whereas America wanted to forego trying some highly-educated medical researchers as war criminals as part of a quiet quid pro quo, the Soviets wanted to make noise.

The request went to MacArthur's headquarters. On February 7, 1947, MacArthur sent a dispatch to Washington: "Prosecutor for USSR at IMTFE (International Military Tribunal Far East) requests permission to interrogate former Japanese General Ishii, Colonel Kikuchi, and Colonel Ota, all formerly connected with Bacteriological Warfare research . . . Request based on information . . . that experiments authorized and conducted by above . . . resulted in deaths of 2000 Chinese and Manchurians."

"Opinion here," MacArthur continued, "that Russians not likely to obtain information from Japanese not already known to United States and that United States might get some additional information from Russian line of questioning in monitored interrogations." The contest of wits and information-maneuvering between America and Russia was on. Should the U.S., MacArthur asked the War Department, acquiesce to the Russian request?

About six weeks later, toward the end of March 1947, permission came from the Joint Chiefs of Staff in Washington for a "SCAP-controlled Soviet interrogation" of Ishii, Kikuchi, and Ota. Before the U.S. let the Soviets get to them, however, Kikuchi and Ota were to be interviewed by competent American personnel. The War Department expressed its readiness to dispatch such personnel to Tokyo for a preliminary interrogation secret from the Soviets, then for monitoring the subsequent Soviet interrogation. If the preliminary interrogations brought out any important facts, the Japanese ex-officers were to be instructed not to reveal them to the Soviets, and also not to tell the Soviets that the preliminary interrogations had taken place. The Americans' line of reasoning in denying the Soviets unfettered access to the prisoners was that war crimes allegedly committed against Chinese did not represent a legitimate war crime interest for the Soviets, and that U.S. permission for the Soviets to conduct investigations should be considered to have been granted purely as a friendly gesture.

MacArthur's office agreed to the dispatch of qualified personnel. Washington then informed SCAP that a Doctor Norbert H. Fell had been selected by the Chemical Warfare Service, and he would leave for Japan in the first week of April. Upon Fell's arrival in Japan, the same Kamei Kan'ichiro who had translated for Sanders pushed his way onto the scene to "assist." Immunity from war crimes had not yet been fully granted, though its possibility was hanging in the air. Kamei was hinting that there were people who had information which would prove of interest to the Americans, but they were not very willing to talk about it for fear of being brought into the trials. And this time, in a reversal of Sanders' tactic against Naito, Kamei made use of the Communist threat against the Americans.

Kamei, according to Fell's report, claimed that he knew people formerly with Unit 731 who were afraid of giving information to the U.S. because the Russians would get hold of it. Holding out the incentive of Japanese silence before Red interrogators, Kamei said that those Japanese felt that the best thing for them now would be to tell Moscow nothing. These pragmatics aside, Kamei also resorted to a pious "we were victims" defense—that the Soviets had been engaging in biological warfare against the Japanese, and "we had to think about defensive measures." Japan, he claimed, knew about Soviet biological warfare work from captured Soviet spies in Manchuria, and there had been no other recourse for Japan but to work on defensive biological warfare. Then, in the course of this research, they had discovered the offensive aspects.

Meanwhile, anonymous and signed reports had been coming in to the American authorities in Tokyo from people who had been victims of the system, enlisted in one unsuspecting way or other into Ishii's research network. A limited few identified themselves, accusing Ishii and Wakamatsu, the veterinarian who had run Unit 100 in Xinjing.

As information started coming into the hands of the American investigators, it came with attempts to conceal the organizational reach of the machinery of human experimentation; even as they confessed, the informants tried to save their own skins. Ishii, it was claimed, was a renegade having nothing to do with the legitimate line of command or military authority. The Japanese medical profession was not involved. The emperor knew nothing. People's consciences may have been smarting and moving them to come clean—but not to the point of suppressing the instinct for self-preservation, or their continuing loyalty to Emperor Hirohito.

Fell met with some twenty people connected with biological warfare. Then, back at Camp Detrick, he compiled the results and conclusions of his mission and stated that the human experimentation conducted by the Japanese would provide valuable data. The Soviets, ever the ping-pong ball in the vying between Washington and Unit 731, appeared again, this time in Fell's report when he quoted Ishii as saying, "My experience would be a useful advantage to the United States in the event of a war with the Soviet Union."

Three days after Fell's last report went off to Major General Alden Waitt, chief of the U.S. Army's Chemical Corps, MacArthur's office messaged the War Department that "Ishii states that if guaranteed immunity from 'War Crimes' in documentary form for himself, superiors and subordinates, he can describe program in detail.

"Ishii claims to have extensive theoretical high-level knowledge including strategic and tactical use of BW on defense and offense, backed by some research on best BW agents to employ by geographical areas of Far East, [and] the use of BW in cold climates."

The viability of bacteria—their ability to survive and thrive—is dependent upon their environment. Differences in the natural environmental conditions of various regions mean that bacteria developed in the United States, for example, may not do well in conditions in Asian areas, which would degrade their effectiveness as weapons. Ishii's statement shows that he had considered bacterial viability in relation to the various areas where his units were functioning. If Asia were to be a continuing area of military operation for the United States, biological weapons developed for Asian environments would be of interest.

The Japanese knew by now that they had little to fear from the Americans in terms of raw hate retribution. During the war, Japanese civilians had been bombed, burned, and irradiated. American conduct from the beginning of the Occupation, though, had consistently demonstrated that the Japanese now would be treated in an orderly and compassionate manner. This feeling of security contrasted directly to what Japanese military leaders feared would happen to them at the hands of victorious Russians and Chinese, whose civilian populations had suffered worse atrocities. A message from Mac-

Arthur to Washington dated May 6, 1947 mentions clearly that "statements so far have been obtained by persuasion, exploitation of Japanese fear of USSR, and desire to cooperate with the US." America was showing interest in matters more practical than turning up defendants for war crimes trials.

(Ironically, the Japanese were not entirely correct about who would mete out the most generous treatment in the wake of the war. The Soviet Union certainly justified Japanese fears of revenge, with tens of thousands of Japanese soldiers dying and disappearing at the hands of the Red Army, as it swept through Manchuria. The Chinese Communists, however, behaved much differently. In the oral history *Japan at War*, by Theodore and Haruko Cook, a former Japanese POW held by the Chinese Communists reports that "there were one thousand sixty-two of us altogether . . . Forty-five of us were indicted and the others were given a reprieve." By contrast, the same book reports that "of 4,000 arrested as war criminals by Allied nations in the Pacific and Asian theaters, 1,068 were executed or died in prison from 1946 to 1951." Another former POW remarks, "I really believe the Chinese Communist Party were the ones who spared my life.")

At this point in time, the question of whom to prosecute in war crimes trials had not been completely settled. Testimony reported by the Soviets was convincing enough for IPS to inform the War Department of its opinion that it "warrants conclusion that Japanese BW group headed by Ishii did violate rules of land warfare, but this expression of opinion is not a recommendation that group be charged and tried for such," adding that corroboration and evaluation of the suspects and their testimony for trustworthiness would be necessary first. In favor of prosecution, MacArthur recognized that high-ranking Japanese liable for prosecution for war crimes were not necessarily the best sources of information. "A large part of data including most of the valuable technical BW information as to results of human experimentation and research in BW for crop destruction probably can be obtained in this manner from low echelon Japanese personnel not believed liable to 'War Crimes' trials."

On the other hand, the general also clearly perceived benefits to be had from pardoning the higher ranking researchers. His feelings on this matter are particularly evident in his advice to the War Department that "additional data, possibly including some statements from Ishii probably can be obtained by informing Japanese involved that information will be retained in intelligence channels and will not be employed as 'War Crimes' evidence." In particular, immunity from prosecution "will result in exploiting the twenty years experience of the director, former General Ishii." Furthermore, acquiring information in this way would prevent it from coming out in courtroom testimony, which would enable the Soviets, among others, to gain access to it. This United States would become the sole recipient of the information.

The same message also contains a brief item advising that adoption of this method was "recommended by CINCFE. [Commander in Chief Far East, or MacArthur]." CINCFE also advised Washington that information including plans and theories of Ishii and his superiors could probably be obtained by granting written guarantees of immunity to Ishii and his associates. Moreover, Ishii could assist in securing the complete cooperation of his former subordinates. All of these ideas suggest that MacArthur strongly supported the idea of determining war crime liability in light of what potential defendants could offer in exchange for amnesty.

It is interesting that in almost all communications between SCAP and Washington concerning these matters, the term "war crimes," with or without capital letters, is enclosed in quotation marks. Critics have said from the day of its inception that the military tribunal was a court of the victors' judging the vanquished, rather than an objective judgment of war crimes. Considering the selectivity with which subjects were chosen for or excluded from trial, the U.S. military's casual treatment of this term suggests that there is more truth to this accusation than many people are willing to acknowledge.

New information also whetted the Americans' appetites for additional data—and spurred them on to try to outmaneuver the Soviets. Actual copies of the Soviet interrogations of Japanese officers who were captured from Ishii's unit in Manchuria were handed over to the American military. MacArthur's headquarters advised the War Department that preliminary investigations "confirm authenticity of USSR interrogations and indicate Japanese activity in (a) Human experimentation. (b) Field trials against Chinese. (c) Large scale program. (d) Research on BW by crop destruction. (e) Possible that Japanese General Staff knew and authorized program. (f) Thought and research devoted to strategic and tactical use of BW . . . [A]bove topics are of great intelligence value to US. Dr. Fell, War Department representative, states that this new evidence was not known by US."

Japanese researchers' experiments with crop destruction attracted particular attention. A list of questions drawn up by the Chemical Corps of the War Department for Dr. Fell to pursue included: "What were the main crops considered for destruction?"; "What field trials were carried out?"; "What kind of equipment had been developed for applying crop destroying materials?"; "What crop diseases do you know or can [you] recognize?"; and "Do any of these [known/recognized diseases] cause serious losses in the vicinity of the BW installation?"

On June 3, 1947, the War Department in Washington communicated with Alva C. Carpenter of the Legal Section of SCAP, asking for detailed information on all possible war crimes evidence or charges against Ishii or any of his group "for consideration in conference here concerning this matter. Specifically what evidence of war crimes is now in possession of the U.S. authorities against Ishii or any member of the group for whom he has requested immunity." Vigilant against threats to its monopoly on the treasure trove of biological warfare knowledge at hand, the War Department also wanted to know which American allies had filed war crimes charges against Ishii or his associates.

Carpenter replied that his section had only anonymous letters, affidavits of hearsay, and rumors on Ishii and his associates. He informed Washington that "the Legal Section interrogations to date of the numerous persons concerned with the BW project in China, do not reveal sufficient evidence to support war crime charges. The alleged victims are of unknown identity. Unconfirmed allegations are to the effect that criminals, farmers, women and children were used for BW experimental purposes." Legal Section noted allegations by the Japanese Communist Party that Ishii and his group "conducted experimentation on captured Americans in Mukden and that simultaneously, research on similar lines was conducted in Tokyo and Kyoto."

Also, according to Legal Section, there was not sufficient evidence on file against any of Ishii's subordinates to charge or hold them as crime suspects. The message did list possible superiors of Ishii who were then on trial, including Tojo and two other former commanders of the Kwantung Army. But neither Ishii nor his associates were listed as war criminals, and no American ally had filed charges of war crimes against them.

SCAP was ready to let Ishii and his associates off the hook. Before the War Department could reach a decision, however, it had to know what opinion IPS held regarding the Ishii biological warfare group. The War Department requested information, and so Legal Section conferred with IPS. The latter body provided a list of biological warfare activities then known to it, and the statement that "strong circumstantial evidence exists of use of bacteria warfare."

By this time, full translations of the affidavits made by a Major Karazawa to his Soviet captors had come into the hands of IPS. In these, it was stated that Karazawa was engaged in the manufacture of germs at the Ishii unit. More specifically, in 1940, Ishii and one hundred of his subordinates had conducted an experimental test in Hangzhou, central China, for which Karazawa claimed he had manufactured seventy kilograms of typhus bacilli, five kilograms of cholera bacilli, and five kilograms of plague-infected fleas. Bacteria were sprayed by plane over areas occupied by the Chinese army, following which a plague epidemic broke out at Ningbo. Karazawa also repeated information he had heard from Ishii about how he had experimented with cholera and plague on the mountain bandits of Manchuria, and that in 1942, when the Japanese army was retreating in central China, the Ishii group infected the vicinity of Chuxian and Yushan with typhoid and plague bacilli. Further testimony claimed that on several occasions during 1943 and 1944, the

Japanese *kenpeitai* had furnished as fodder for human experimentation with plague and anthrax bacilli Manchurians "who had been sentenced to death." Karazawa even implicated people at the very top of Japan's military organization, claiming that Ishii had advised his staff that they were under orders from the General Staff in Tokyo to improve virus research.

IPS had also obtained information on four locations in China where, in October and November of 1940, Japanese planes scattered wheat grains, and bubonic plague appeared shortly afterward. Yet, it still refrained from bringing Ishii to trial. Nor did it deem it worthwhile to call up members of the Ishii group to testiify against their superiors who were listed as defendants in the trials. In December 1946, after considering using the material in its hands as a basis for prosecution, IPS replied to SCAP, and by extension the War Department, that the evidence on hand was not sufficient to connect any of the accused with the Ishii detachments's secret activities. Its reply to SCAP and the War Department back in Washington, was couched along these lines.

Some copies of these reports were labeled as being destined for the "Commander in Chief," so there can be little doubt that the U.S. president was informed of events in Tokyo, including the biological warfare intelligence coming into America's hands. In other words—to borrow the expression that that president himself made famous—on the decision not to prosecute the former members of Unit 731, the buck stopped right at Harry Shippe Truman's desk.

America's decision not to prosecute Ishii and his men was not the final word on the matter, however. In July 1948, the Soviet army newspaper *Red Star* carried an article by a Col. Galkin, special correspondent on the newspaper for Japanese biological warfare. According to the article, the Japanese were preparing to use biological warfare on a large scale, and they had a huge bacteriological center in Manchuria. Galkin's piece did not state that Japanese biological warfare was intended for use against his country, and instead specifically pointed out that it was for use against China, the United States, and Britain. The *Red Star* article also did not mention Soviet citizens as victims of human experimentation. Still more surprising, the Soviet article did not mention the imperial order which had allegedly led to the establishment of the labs. There was only mention of Prince Mikasa acting as the emperor's representative.

Some time later, however, a different version of events emerged from behind the Iron Curtain. In December 1949, in the city of Khabarovsk, on the railway line north of Vladivostok, twelve former members of Ishii's organization were placed on trial for war crimes. Soviet press reports told the U.S. State Department of the first installment of the trial results, and included "confessions" by several Japanese that the Japanese General Staff and War Ministry had set up secret labs in Manchuria in 1935–1936, for preparation and execution of bacteriological warfare. During court testimony, these were said to have been established on direct order from Emperor Hirohito. The Soviet account goes on to state that the Soviet Union was one of the intended targets of Japan's biological warfare efforts, that Soviet citizens were among the victims of experimental research, that bacteria were mass-produced for use in war, and that outposts along the Soviet border were established for the purpose of conducting biological warfare against the U.S.S.R.

Soviet veracity was brought into question, as the State Department compared these accounts of the trial with the Red Army newspaper's earlier recounting of biological warfare activities. It is apparent that Moscow had hoped to use the *Red Star* article as a goad (assisted by the fact that the *New York Times* picked up the story, too, and brought it wide publicity back in the United States): how could the other Allies—specifically the U.S.—refuse to bring the former members of Unit 731 to trial when their own citizens had been victimized? The timing of the Russian trial, and the accounts of it, in which no special pains were taken to emphasize Japan's use of biological warfare against countries other than the Soviet Union, supports this viewpoint. The Tokyo war crimes trials had been wrapped up four months after the appearance of the *Red Star* article without Ishii or his cohorts ever making an appearance, and so the Soviets no longer had any incentive to dwell on any suffering other than their own.

America wanted Ishii, Ishii's group, and the emperor protected. More than that, it wanted secrecy and exclusivity. The Soviets pressed to bring them all to trial, so that the secrets America had obtained from the Japanese could be made available to everyone (especially them). America won. And Unit 731 made its contribution to the Cold War. One might raise the question of what role the transfer of Japan's biological warfare potential to the U.S. played in pushing the Soviets to outdo America in nuclear capability. Again, Japanese-American collusion has prevented the question from being asked.

5
Unit 731 in Modern Times

It is impossible to exaggerate the secrecy enveloping information about Unit 731 in the postwar era. As recently as June 26, 1995, the *Japan Times* reported that "a woman in Sendai . . . has recently discovered a résumé written by her late father showing that he worked for the secret Japanese army which researched germ warfare in China during World War II." The story of Unit 731 was not even handed down from parents to children (at least among the unit's erstwhile members).

It should therefore be unsurprising that the history of Unit 731 has remained at the farthest periphery of Japan's collective consciousness since the end of the war. Yet, as in the case of the frostbite specialist Dr. Yoshimura, former upper-level members of the unit, together with their cooperating medical researchers in Japan, made great—and quiet—use of their data to further their careers in Japanese academia, science, industry, and politics. Still, the postwar history of Unit 731 is not confined to the stories of those former members who used their experience for their own personal gain. Like an invisible yet undeniably present ghost, the defunct outfit has continued to stalk Japan—and the world—in other ways, as well.

The Teikoku Bank Incident

In January 1948, a man walked into a branch of the Teikoku Bank ("Teigin," short for *Teikoku Ginko*) in Tokyo and identified himself as an official of the Ministry of Health and Welfare. He advised the bank manager that there was an epidemic in the area, and that all employees were requested to drink a preventive medicine that he had brought with him. It was good medicine, he reassured the banker, and his ministry had received it from GHQ (General Headquarters, Douglas MacArthur's office) itself. The manager dutifully gathered all employees of the bank for instructions.

The so-called representative inserted a pipette into the liquid contents of a bottle he had brought and drew some off into a teacup. He demonstrated how the tongue should be extended first so that the liquid would go quickly and directly into the throat, then drank the substance in front of the employees. Next, he took a quantity of the liquid from the same bottle into each of sixteen cups, one for each person present. He instructed them to drink this in unison when he gave the word. Then, after a wait of one minute—which he would time precisely by his watch—they were to drink a second medicine. They all obediently followed his instructions. Twelve employees died, while the other four recovered to bear witness.

While the criminal's modus operandi—poison as a robbery weapon—was odd to begin with, even odder was the crime's seeming lack of a motive. The murderer took a total of ¥181,850 which was lying on some of the desks, but left much more untouched. It thus became apparent that some purpose other than robbery had brought him to the bank.

Vexed at the peculiar nature of this crime, the police searched for suspects. Descriptions provided by the four survivors of the poisoning enabled law enforcement authorities to create the first montage photo in Japan. The photo, in turn, helped lead to the arrest of an artist by the name of Hirasawa Sadamichi.

After being thoroughly grilled, and attempting suicide in prison, Hirasawa confessed. His confession, however, was less than convincing. His written statement, for example, claimed that "the poison was in a bottle similar in shape to a beer bottle, so I poured the substance from the bottle directly into the glasses." The bottles he carried were not shaped like beer bottles, according to the survivors, but wide-mouthed jars. And in describing the drinking vessels, he used the Japanese-Dutch word *koppu,* used in Japan to mean "drinking glass." Japanese-style teacups, from which the survivors said they drank, are referred to by another term.

Another discrepancy is that the murderer used a pipette to transfer the substance from the bottle to each teacup. This, in fact, is how investigators assumed he duped his victims into thinking that he drank the same substance first. A harmless oil could easily be floated on the surface of the poison, and a pipette inserted into this top layer would draw off only the oil; subsequent insertions of the pipette would be deeper, so that the tube went beneath the oil layer and sucked out the poison underneath.

At the time of the incident, Japanese law considered a confession proof of guilt; apparently, there was nothing other than his confession to support belief in his guilt.

Even survivors brought in to view Hirasawa in a police lineup said he did not resemble the man who came to the bank. Soon after the Teigin Incident, the law was changed so that a confession on its own would not be considered a reasonable standard of proof to convict a defendant. In contemporary times, there would probably not be enough evidence against Hirasawa to convict him.

Even the evidence that the state did have proved troublesome—and suspect. Keio University and Tokyo University each performed autopsies on six of the twelve victims chosen at random. Keio found that the poison was acetone cyanohydrin. Two to three months later, Tokyo University issued its findings: the poison was potassium cyanide. The sequence of events surrounding the release of these conflicting autopsy reports is one of the elements that casts an ever darker shadow over the findings, and strengthens suspicions of the incident's connection with Unit 731. The Keio results naming the murder poison as acetone cyanohydrin were released before Hirasawa was arrested. Then, some two to three months after Hirasawa's arrest, Tokyo University came out with its findings that the poison used was potassium cyanide.

The type of poison used in the crime was a crucial factor in determining the direction in which the finger of accusation would point. Potassium cyanide was a poison with a long history, and it would not be unavailable to someone who really wanted it. An instantaneously acting poison, it would have been unsuitable for a sabotage-style operation: the victim would succumb immediately upon ingesting the poison, and the identity of the poisoner would be obvious. Accordingly, the Tokyo University findings left room for suspicion.

On the other hand, acetone cyanohydrin was a poison

with a much different history and set of characteristics. The Japanese army had been searching for a poison that would not take effect until a short time after the victim drank it. It had tackled this problem at Noborito Army Research Center in Kawasaki, a laboratory for developing special weapons operating under the same secret army umbrella as Unit 731. Ishii's unit worked closely with Noborito by conducting human tests for products under development. Acetone cyanohydrin was produced under the Noborito poison development program. It had been tested on Chinese prisoners by the Ishii organization under the same ruse used at Teigin, the claim that it was a preventive medicine against a communicable disease. The test produced death in five to six minutes. Provocative, too, was the fact that two boxes of acetone cyanohydrin had disappeared from the Noborito laboratory in the confusion attending the end of the war.

At the time of the incident, acetone cyanohydrin was not a garden-variety poison like potassium cyanide. It was available only to a very select handful of people—those working at Noborito, and relevant personnel attached to Unit 731. It is highly unlikely that someone like Hirasawa could ever have gotten his hands on it. If acetone cyanohydrin was, in fact, the poison used in the crime, then Hirasawa would be an unlikely suspect. If, on the other hand, the poison were potassium cyanide after all, then Hirasawa could be as suspect as anyone else.

One question that naturally occurs and recurs is, Why would Hirasawa confess if he were innocent? Investigators into his background turned up evidence that he had been diagnosed as suffering from Korsakoff's Syndrome. This aberrant condition is characterized by irregular memory loss, for which the patient tries to compensate by creating falsehoods. A bigger and more important question, however, is this: Why did the two universities produce such completely different autopsy results?

The head of the Japanese police investigation into the case reported to the occupation forces that the modus operandi in the Teigin murders bore a "similarity to the training received at the Arsenal [Noborito] laboratory." For that matter, Ishii himself, in one of his interrogation sessions with American military officers, commented on the Teigin murders, "I have the feeling that one of my men did it." These clues pointed the police in the direction of Japan's old biological warfare program, and the police investigation started by zeroing in on former Unit 731 members. A list of suspects was drawn up, and trails led to the army laboratory.

Then, almost overnight, the direction of the investigation reversed and homed in on Hirasawa; the army laboratory vanished from the radar screens of law enforcement officials. It goes without saying that the Japanese authorities did not want an investigation that would end up publicizing Unit 731 to the outside world. More to the point, though, it is equally obvious that this change in investigative direction served the interests of the American military authorities, since it prevented the Ishii organization from emerging into the spotlight that Washington and SCAP had so vigorously tried to keep it out of.

The U.S. and Japanese governments' reluctance to consider a possible Unit 731 role in the Teigin Incident would help provide a motive for falsification of the Tokyo University test results, if that is in fact what happened. Tokyo University had strong connections with the Ishii organization, supplying many of the doctors, researchers, and students to the units in China, and working with data provided through human experimentation. This elite (and government-overseen) school also has firm links with Japan's ruling class. Most Japanese politicians at the national level are Tokyo University graduates, and the school could be influenced by government pressure much more easily than Keio, a private university. Critics also point out that it is easier for a court to hand down a judgment that agrees with the police and public prosecutor. Once the accusation focused on Hirasawa, it had to be supported by the discovery of a means of murder available to him. The secretly produced, generally unknown, and unavailable acetone cyanohydrin did not fit the needs of those who sought to convict Hirasawa.

In the end, the judgment was handed down that the substance was potassium cyanide and Hirasawa was guilty. He was sentenced to death, but the paper which would have ordered his execution into effect was not stamped. It never was stamped through all the years that he spent in prison. Nobody wanted that responsibility. Hirasawa spent more than three decades under a death penalty that was never put into effect.

Appalled at this apparent miscarriage of justice in which the evidence had been molded to fit the desired judgment, a small group of people pressed for a reexamination of the case. Their efforts to obtain a retrial continued all the way to the time of Hirasawa's death in jail in 1987, at the age of ninety-five. Today, the Teigin poisoning incident is a mystery that continues to provoke sporadic interest among Japanese. Some researchers into the crime go so far as to suspect that the murders were a postwar extension of Unit 731 activity. To them, the very careful one-minute timing between the first and second liquids was a possible reaction-time test. (This hypothesis posits that the second liquid was not necessarily anything poisonous, but just a decoy to give the criminal an

excuse for timing his experiment.) This view is supported by rumors that the U.S. occupation forces were involved and that the bank employees were used as human
test subjects. Along these lines, stories also circulated of
a GHQ car's having been in the vicinity when the incident took place. These claims are unsubstantiated,
though, and seem closer to the category of gossip than
decisive proof.

Nonetheless, all the other, reliable evidence leads one
to think that there is still more to this story than has yet
met the eye. And if a true version of events ever is proven,
it may well show up the official conclusion in the Teigin
Incident as nothing but a piece of fiction. Future investigation may someday reveal that the post-World War II
ghost of the Ishii unit lurked somewhere nearby, after all.

Japanese Biological Warfare Data in the Korean War

In March 1951, about half a year after Red China's
People's Liberation Army entered into the Korean War,
Beijing reported that United Nations forces were resort-
ing to biological warfare in the field. On May 8, 1951,
Park Hen Yen, foreign minister of the Democratic People's Republic of Korea (North Korea), lodged an official
protest with the United Nations. U.S. forces, he claimed,
had attacked Pyongyang with smallpox. This was denied
by the U.N. commander. In February of the following
year, a new accusation came from North Korea that, for
the past month, Americans had been systematically scat-
tering large quantities of bacteria-carrying insects by
aircraft, targeting North Korean army positions. China's
premier and minister of foreign affairs, Zhou Enlai, lodged
a separate and similar protest against the U.S. on Febru-

ary 24; in doing so, he directly lent his country's prestige to the North Korean accusation. He further asserted that the Americans had first started using biological warfare even earlier than the North Koreans had claimed, starting in December 1950. The protests were picked up on by other Communist countries, which, as usual, saw an opportunity for scoring propaganda points.

Naturally, North Korea's other major patron, the Soviet Union, got involved, condemning America's alleged use of biological warfare weaponry. America, the Soviets reminded the world, was the only member of the Security Council which had not ratified the 1925 Geneva Protocol outlawing biological and chemical weapons in war. America rejoined that the protocol was obsolete and only a paper promise (after all, what good had it done in restraining the Japanese, who *were* signatories?), and that the U.S.S.R. was merely committed to a policy of "no first use," something that they could get around at any time by claiming that the other side acted first. Finally, the U.N. offered to have the International Red Cross investigate on both sides. This proposal, however, only brought accusations from North Korea that the organization was merely a tool of American aggression and a spy agency.

In the absence of concrete proof of biological warfare by the United States, the overwhelming majority of U.N. member nations rejected the accusations. U.N. commander Matthew B. Ridgeway countered by dismissing the Communist accusations as a coverup for the inability on the part of China and North Korea to handle the epidemics that break out seasonally within their borders.

If these allegations were true, they would certainly serve as further evidence of the U.S. military's having acquired the results of Unit 731 research and field tests in what one could reasonably assume was a tradeoff for immunity from prosecution. There were also rumors in Japan about former Unit 731 members going to Korea with the American forces. A bomb on permanent display in the Unit 731 Museum in Manchuria that was one of the items on loan to Japan for the exhibitions carried a description tag stating that it was found in Korea. There is, of course, no proof that this is the case, and the bomb could very well have been recovered in some area of China where the Japanese dropped it during World War II, then recycled during the Korean conflict by the Communists for new propaganda purposes.

On the other hand, epidemic hemorrhagic fever—the disease with which Kitano Masaji did his best-known work—was not endemic to Korea before the Korean War, and yet more than 2,600 cases of it were reported among U.S. troops during three years of the conflict. Of these, 165 people died. When the disease first struck the U.S. Army in 1951, it was practically unknown to Western medicine. Some research on it had been carried out in the Soviet Union, but Unit 731, with all its experience in developing it as a tool for offensive warfare, was the world authority on the disease.

U.S. Army researchers looked to former Unit 731 members for help in dealing with the problem. In the *Annals of Internal Medicine* for 1953, Colonel Joseph H. McNinch, U.S. Army Medical Corps and Chief of Preventive Medicine, Far East Command, writes, "At this time [summer 1951], attention was directed toward a disease which the Japanese Army had encountered in Manchuria in 1939–1941, and which was written up in Japanese medical literature." In other reports, written by researchers with the U.S. Army Medical Corps, the names of some ten former Unit 731 members, including Kitano, appear.

Another U.S. Army medical officer's report on his work with former Unit 731 members and EHF includes the comment that, according to information provided by the Japanese, research in Manchuria ended with the end of World War II, and "the transmissible agent was lost at the time of surrender." If it was *not* lost—there was only the word of the Japanese researchers to support the claim that it was—did it reappear in Korea through some sort of secret collaboration between Occupation authorities and Japan's biological warfare experts?

This conveniently timed outbreak in Korea of a disease in which Unit 731 was the world's leading storehouse of knowledge, and other already-documented postwar cooperation between that outfit and the Americans, suggests that Unit 731's role in the Korean War was not simply confined to controlling and curing the disease. Rather, the facts available appear to encourage the belief that the Americans, assisted by their former Japanese enemies, carried out against the North Koreans biological warfare attacks which ended up backfiring.

Meanwhile, the Manchurian bomb from China's Unit 731 museum continues posing the question of whether it is mere Red propaganda, or a relic of U.S.-Unit 731 collaboration in the Korean War.

Shinjuku Shock

In the 1980s, Tokyo decided to center its municipal functions in Shinjuku Ward, and the area experienced a construction boom of hotels and government buildings. Shinjuku represented all the well-worn compliments paid

to active localities. It was growing, moving ahead, looking to the future—and then Shinjuku shocked Japan
back into the past. In June 1989, large quantities of
human bones were unearthed at a construction excava-
tion site for a new facility of the Ministry of Health and
Welfare. The location was at the site of the former Army
Medical College, where Ishii had lectured on his experiments and displayed preserved human specimens brought
in from Unit 731. Ironically, police investigations concluded that there was no violent crime involved, and
plans were made to cremate the bones. At that point,
however, activist citizens put pressure on the ward government to scrutinize the matter further. There was strong
reason to believe that the bones were remains from Unit
731's human experiments, and some people in Japan
wanted an investigation.

The citizens' group pressed the ward head to expedite
identification of the bones. The ward head, in turn,
asked the assistance of medical and scientific institutions
within the ward, including the National Science Museum; all refused for reasons which the involved citizens
interpret as government pressure.

Some two years after the discovery, Dr. Sakura Hajime,
an anthropologist, retired from the National Science
Museum and joined Sapporo Gakuin University, where
he received permission to go ahead with the identification of the bones. On April 22, 1992, he announced his
findings. The *Asahi* newspaper carried an article on his
results the following day: the bones dated back "from
several tens of, to one hundred years" earlier. Other
discoveries in the course of the investigation included the
facts that: the bones were from more than one hundred
people; the ratio of males to females was three to one;
skulls made up the major part of the remains; and the

DECLASSIFIED PER EXECUTIVE ORDER 12356, SECTION 3.3, NND PROJECT
NUMBER 832469 , BY RLB/CR9 , DATE 3/27/95

THE GAIMUSHO
TOKYO

February 3, 1950

Dear Mr. Sebald,

Concerning the Soviet demand for international trial of the Emperor and the bacteriological warfare alleged to have been waged by the Kwantung army the Prime Minister has instructed me to inquire if your office has any information beyond what has been carried by the press.

I want to call on you. Please, let me know what time it will be most convenient to you.

Yours sincerely

The Honorable
Mr. W.J. Sebald

Diplomatic Section
GHQ, SCAP.
Tokyo.

Vice Minister for Foreign
Affairs.

Soviet demands that Emperor Hirohito face trial for war crimes caused the Japanese great distress, as this recently (1995) released note from the Foreign Ministry to SCAP shows.

Pingfang's double chimney looms ominously over the complex grounds.

Restoration efforts are currently underway in Pingfang, shown here in recent times.

This building had refrigeration units used for freezing human beings all year round.

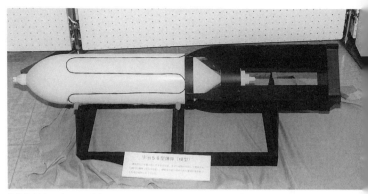

Ishii Shiro himself developed the Uji-50 bacterial bomb.

China claims this bomb was dropped in Korea by the U.S. in the Korean War.

131

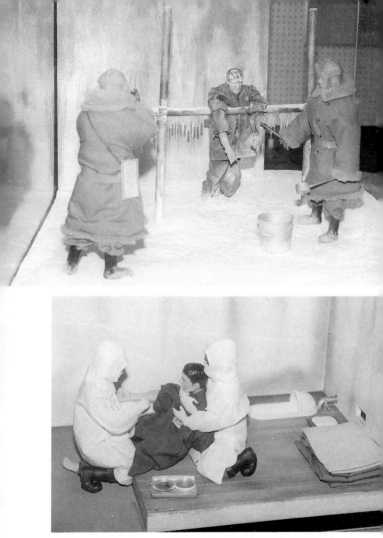

Replicas of experiments displayed at the Unit 731 Exhibition.
(Above) Water is poured over the victim's limbs in subfreezing
temperatures. *(Below)* A prisoner in a single cell is forcibly injected
with pathogens. *(Right)* A team of doctors dissects a victim; one
member weighs organs removed from the body.

Rats were raised by Youth Corps members in cells like these.

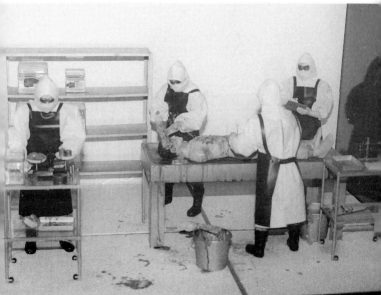

At Takatsuki, Naganuma Setsuji *(detail)* remembers his wartime days.

Former Unit 731 nurse Akama Masako speaks at Takatsuki.
To her right is author Nishino Rumiko.

Exhibition participants explain the exhibits to visitors.

bones were "nearly all Mongoloid in origin, but of several groups, and it is highly possible that Chinese, Koreans, and Japanese are represented."

Some of the skulls had drill holes or had been cut with a saw. All of these procedures had been performed after the deaths of their subjects, suggesting that these people had been used as materials for medical instruction. Some skulls bore signs of ear surgery practice, while others bore "signs similar to brain surgery practice." The report also stated that many of the bones showed a strong possibility of previous preservation as specimens.

At a press conference reported in the same *Asahi* article, the ward head stated that the ethnic backgrounds of the bones could not be accurately identified, and that while the bones showed signs of use in medical instruction, no association had been established with the experiments of Unit 731. The ward's position, in conclusion, was that "since there is nobody [i.e., relatives] who can claim the remains, the ward wants to cremate them."

The citizens' group, on the other hand, interpreted Dr. Sakura's results as evidence that supported and even exceeded their suspicions, and they called for a halt to the cremation. They also demanded further investigation by the ward, the city, and the national government. Such an investigation has not materialized, but neither have the bones been burned. They currently remain in the possession of a funeral home in Shinjuku.

The episode made an impact on the international stage, as well. In December 1994, Japan asked the United States Postal Service to cancel its plans to issue a postage stamp commemorating the atomic bomb explosion over Hiroshima. Sensitive to requests to "respect Japan's national feelings," the U.S. subsequently abandoned the stamp plan, replacing it with a stamp memorializing President Harry Truman. Seizing upon this incident, China's official *People's Daily* newspaper published an editorial criticizing Japan for objecting to the American stamp plan while Japan itself had (and has) still not faced up to its own past aggression in China. The number of victims in the atomic bombings of Japan and in the Rape of Nanjing were about equal, the paper stated, and yet "the atomic bomb was the result of Japanese militarism, while the Rape of Nanjing was the result of Japan's invading China." The newspaper criticized the Shinjuku officials for trying to burn the bones quickly, and pointed to the activities of the Shinjuku citizens' group as an example of the mutual respect which is necessary for achieving peace. It is interesting to note that the editorial, whose tone was surprisingly non-vindictive, appeared in the newspaper's domestic edition, but not in its overseas one.

The May 1994 edition of *Tokyo Journal* carried an interview with Professor Tsuneishi Keiichi, the noted researcher into Unit 731, in which he spoke of family members who are interested in further identification of the remains found at the Tokyo construction site. Some, he stated, have written letters, which were personally delivered by members of the Shinjuku citizens' group to the Ministry of Foreign Affairs. Then, in 1993, according to Tsuneishi, members of the same citizens' group went to Harbin and invited one of the relatives to attend the Unit 731 Exhibition in Japan. With the assistance of the group, the woman whom they invited tried to visit the Ministry of Health, which refused to receive her, or allow her to view the bones.

As far back as 1945, the Japanese government has consistently denied that the Japanese army conducted human experiments and biological warfare. Admitting now that the bones are from Unit 731's victims would amount to the admission of a half-century's worth of lies. It would also raise the problem of compensation. Yet, until Japan makes some sort of concrete acknowledgment of what it did during the war, it seems consigned to permanent ostracism. In what could seem like a pathetically small act of revenge from the grave, the victims may be thought of as having returned, years after they were put to their agonizing deaths, to create minor torture for Japan's political elite.

The Unit Leaders in Peacetime

By virtue, ostensibly, of their cooperation with their American conquerors, the former leadership of Unit 731 lived relatively quietly and undisturbed in the postwar period. The freedom they enjoyed stands in stark contrast to the fates of other, better-known "Class A" war criminals, such as Prime Minister Tojo Hideki and General Yamashita Tomoyuki (known as the "Tiger of Malaya" for his conquest of British Singapore), both of whom went to the gallows. Memories of the "good war" fought by America and her allies, and the justice they meted out at Nuremburg and Tokyo, can only provoke ironic smiles when recalled in juxtaposition to the happy lives these men led after the smoke of war had cleared.

Ishii

Ishii Shiro spent his last years in relative and unwilling inactivity. He was afraid of being taken by the Soviets for war crimes, and after negotiating his way into immunity with U.S. authorities, he could not locate meaningful work. His lack of what would today be called "people skills" made him unwelcome to many of his former subordinates who had moved on to lucrative positions of respect, and preferred to distance themselves from Ishii. He wanted to work at Naito Ryoichi's company, but he was not wanted there, either.

Ishii contracted throat cancer—there were rumors of former unit members having a hand in it—and died in 1959 at sixty-nine years of age. Kitano Masaji officiated at his funeral.

Naito Ryoichi, Kitano Masaji, and Futagi Hideo

The American military action in Korea brought a demand for blood. Hearing opportunity knocking, Naito, Kitano, and Futagi decided to go into business together, establishing Japan's first blood bank in 1951. Heavy purchases by the armed forces of the United States set the company on the road to financial success. The blood bank was later named *Midori Juji,* or "Green Cross," and it continued along its prosperous path. It is now one of Japan's leading pharmaceutical companies, and has even moved overseas, setting up offices in the United States.

In February 1988, U.S. medical researchers identified eighteen patients in Japan who had become infected with the AIDS virus through transfusions of infected blood products exported from the United States by Green Cross. The following May, two of the infected patients brought suit against the company (and other related ones). Dr. Yamaguchi Ken'ichiro, a medical practitioner who lectures on Unit 731 and its effect on Japanese medicine today, has stated in his talks his belief that the company knowingly imported and distributed AIDS-tainted blood as part of its program for developing an AIDS vaccine. Successful development of such a medicine would mean astronomical profits. Government approval to market a new substance, however, is difficult to obtain without a history of successful use on humans.

Commenting further on connections between AIDS and biological warfare, Dr. Yamaguchi adds his voice to the chorus of those who find it hard to believe the orthodox explanation that the disease started with monkeys. It is much easier, he says, to think that it was developed in Fort Detrick as part of their ongoing biological warfare program, after which it somehow leaked out. A researcher at Fort Detrick was said to have remarked to the effect that, within ten years, the U.S. would have developed a biological weapon that would be more devastating than anything to date. Just ten years after that statement, the first AIDS case appeared. The Fort Detrick origin, says Yamaguchi, is a much more scientifically realistic explanation.

Postwar Careers: Plum Positions

One of the former unit members described Unit 731 in a postwar interview as the "best paying job" anyone could have gotten at the time. During the days when human experimentation was being carried out, researchers were paid as civilian employees of the Imperial Japanese Army. After the war, this lucrative tradition continued, as payments were made to anyone who had been in any way connected with the units. No official explanation came with the money, and the source was a matter of speculation. The most accepted version of events was that the money was from the U.S. military. It would, after all, represent a bargain sum, considering the value that Washington attached to the data it had received.

Here is a very brief list of what became of some of Unit

731's major players during the postwar years. Each person's wartime research specialty and/or unit affiliation is indicated in parentheses. An asterisk indicates that the person supported the work of Unit 731 as a civilian employee, receiving payment through the Army Laboratory in Tokyo.

Amitani Shogo* (Tokyo University Laboratory for Communicable Diseases)
    Remained attached to same facility after the war and received the Asahi Prize for outstanding scientific performance
Ando Koji (Head, Dalian Laboratory)
    Professor, Tokyo University Laboratory for Communicable Diseases
    Head, Central Laboratory for Experimental Animals
Asahina Masajiro (Typhus vaccine production team)
    National Institute of Health
Futagi Hideo (Vivisection team leader)
    Cofounder, Green Cross Corporation
Kasuga Tadayoshi (Dalian Laboratory)
    Kitasato Research Laboratory
    Ministry of Education, Pertussis (Whooping cough) Research Team
Kimura Yasushi* (Professor, Kyoto University)
    Assistant head, Japan Medical Association
    President, Nagoya City University of Medicine
Kitano Masaji (EHF research, frostbite research)
    Cofounder, Green Cross Corporation
    Special Committee for Antarctic Research
    Ministry of Education, Pertussis Research Team
Kobayashi Rokuzo* (Professor, Keio University)
    Director, First Division, National Institute of Health

Kojima Saburo* (Tokyo University Laboratory for Communicable Diseases)
  Director, Second Division, National Institute of Health
Miyagawa Yoneji* (Head, Tokyo University Laboratory for Communicable Diseases)
  Toshiba Biophysics and Biochemistry Research Laboratory
Murata Yoshisuke (Nanjing, Unit 1644)
  National Institute of Health
Naito Ryoichi (Bacteriological research)
  Cofounder, Green Cross Corporation
Ogata Tomio* (Assistant professor, Tokyo University Laboratory for Communicable Diseases)
  Professor, Faculty of Medicine, Tokyo University
Ogawa Toru (Nanjing, Unit 1644)
  Professor, Faculty of Medicine, Nagoya City University
Okamoto Kozo (Pathology research team)
  Dean, Faculty of Medicine, Kyoto University
  Dean, Faculty of Medicine, Kinki University
Sonoguchi Tadao (Biological warfare development)
  Vice-principal, School of Hygiene of the Japan Self-Defense Forces.
Tanaka Hideo (Plague-carrying fleas team)
  Dean, Faculty of Medicine, Osaka City University
Toda Shozo* (Professor, Kyoto University)
  Member of the Special Committee for Antarctic Research
  President, Kanazawa University
Yanagizawa Ken* (Tuberculosis research team)
  Head, (5th) National Institute of Health

PART

2

TESTIMONIES

Introduction

The Unit 731 Exhibition started touring Japan in July 1993, and continued through December 1994. During that period of approximately one and a half years, it was presented at sixty-one locations. Some materials were borrowed from China, where a permanent memorial museum has been established. Actual photographs of the units are very rare, due to (alleged) destruction or the fact that they remain hidden in private or official corners. Much of the exhibition consisted of written, explanatory panels. This paucity of photographic and other graphic material itself points to a surprising result of the exhibit: organizers of the various local exhibitions repeatedly noted that, despite the large amount of written material on display, people took the time to read.

This eagerness and receptivity with which people attended the exhibition, in turn, leads to another question, simultaneously encouraging and troubling. Do the Japanese people, as is often asserted, really want to be ignorant of their country's checkered past? Or is it just their textbook-censoring leadership that wishes for them to remain so?

At the venues of the Unit 731 Exhibition, visitors were

invited to write their impressions and comments. One sixteen-year-old high school student wrote that he had

> read books and articles on Unit 731, but this was my first time hearing talks by those who actually experienced it. In that sense, coming here today was extremely good. From the time I was in elementary school, I had heard stories from people who experienced bombing raids during the Pacific War. But even though we hear from various sources about our being victims of war, there is almost no talk about Japan's being an assailant. It is important to tell the story from both sides; especially to us in the generation that does not know war, the words of those who did experience it are most valuable. That is why it would be good to increase the places where these words could be heard.
>
> It took about two hours to come here from my home. If I hadn't come I would not have been able to hear these talks.

It is the intention of the author to enable to reader, as best as possible, to share the experience of those who, like that high school student, were impressed and shocked by the words of those who were involved.

Some of these recollections were tape-recorded at exhibition sites. Others came from booklets of the testimonies which were printed up afterward by the various localities where the exhibitions were staged, largely as a volunteer effort.

Not all the speakers felt free to identify themselves. After living with their secrets for fifty years, a reversal of behavior had to come in stages. For most of the people testifying, this was the first stage.

Speaking of these things for the first time in front of people, they reached back in time to reconstruct an ugly past while peeling down emotional barriers layered on through a half-century of silence. These catharses did not always come smoothly, and thoughts are sometimes left ragged by emotions. As a result, some narratives may seem a bit disjointed at times. Despite this tendency, however, meanings and sentiments come through with painful clarity.

Persons are identified with the information available, or with that which they permitted. In some cases, it was relatives who wished for the speakers to keep their identities—and those of their families—confidential. In other cases, half a century was not yet enough to provide a completely healing balm for the scars left by Unit 731.

Researcher attached to Unit 1644 (Anonymous)

[The person who provided this testimony is compiling an account of his experiences at Unit 1644. He and his family are not yet in agreement about his releasing his name, and this excerpt was offered with that understanding.]

I was working as a civilian employee at the Army Medical College in Tokyo. In July 1942, I was transferred to China, and the following month I was assigned to Unit 1644 in Nanjing. In October 1944, I became a member of the army as an enlisted man in the Hygiene Corps.

An associated unit of Unit 731 was set up in Nanjing shortly after that city fell into Japanese hands. Equipment and people were transferred from Harbin. Facilities were great; we even had a swimming pool. The grounds and buildings were superior, of a quality not to be found in Japan. Under the regime of Jiang Jieshi, this had originally been a people's hospital. The front of the hospital complex extended two hundred meters, cut off by a high wall with a guard gate for egress. The grounds extended about seven hundred meters back from this front wall, and there was a large red cross at the top of the main building.

Some buildings left over from earlier times served as facilities like a glass factory and a print shop. One part of the compound was made into a ranch for animals. A running creek separated the animal area from the rest of the compound, and kept the animals from wandering outside the ranch. There was a bridge with a gate over the creek for people to cross over.

Unit 1644 was classified as a battalion, but our budget was the same as that normally allotted to a regiment.

People working in the unit were military doctors, medical specialists, interpreters, and civilian employees.

Our activities included developing preventative vaccines, tending the animals, and drawing the animals' blood for vaccine research and production. A water purification team carried equipment out to different areas for water treatment. I was assigned to the vaccine group. There were one hundred twenty of us, about ten percent of the total complement of the unit. Every day, I would be given information on the previous day's work, including which army doctor performed what work, what results had been obtained, and so forth. I had the job of writing down all these details in a research statement, then I stamped it "secret" and locked it in a safe.

One day a Chinese man tried to take the written records. He was caught and arrested. Shortly afterward, an officer came from Japan, and I was promised an award; the war ended before I had a chance to get it.

Everyone connected with human experiments wore a special button on the side of his hat. The *maruta* were kept in cages on the top floor of a three-story building. The cages were referred to as *rotsu* [probably from the Japanese katakana character *ro,* which is square in shape; the prison block at Pingfang was called *rogo* for this reason], and the floor where they were kept was always just called the "third floor."

One had to pass through the main offices in order to get to the third floor, where the cages were. The area where the prisoners were was sealed off with a door. One meter in front of the door and on its other side were disinfectant mats to prevent bacteriological contaminants from being carried outside on people's shoes.

Inside the door, the room was about ten by fifteen

meters with cages all in a row. Most of the *maruta* in the cages were just lying down. In the same room were oil cans with mice that had been injected with plague germs, and with fleas feeding on the mice. These were not the usual types of fleas, but a transparent variety. Around the perimeter of the room was a thirty-centimeter-wide trough of running water. [The purpose of the trough, which is wider than the distance over which the fleas can leap, is apparently to keep the fleas from going outside the room.]

Next to the dissection room was the specimen room. Every year, when the new soldiers came in, the first job they got was cleaning up at night around the human specimen room. The other soldiers would put a dish of fireflies in the specimen room by the window facing the corridor. The fireflies swarming around the specimens of body parts created an eerie feeling, and some of the young recruits suffered emotional problems from the experience.

❋

Virologist attached to Unit 731 (Anonymous)

In 1934, I graduated Kyoto Prefectural University of Medicine. I then continued my research, specializing in virology. Ishii came on one of his trips to Kyoto looking for people to join him as civilian employees at the Army Medical College in Tokyo. One of the people he recruited was Okamoto Kozo. He gathered some people, but there were no virus specialists among them. Among those who went with Ishii were some of my acquaintances who had been senior to me in earlier days at university, so I joined also and became a civilian employee with pay and status equivalent to an army first lieutenant. I became qualified as an army lab technician, then, in 1939, I was transferred to the unit at Harbin. In 1942, as soon as Singapore was taken over by the Japanese army, I was sent there to help in setting up a unit. I was there until October 1944, when I was sent back to Japan and assigned by the Ministry of Education to teach bacteriology at the Yamanashi Prefectural University of Medicine.

At one stage, I worked at an important post in Yokohama studying the control of viruses in a range of temperatures. We worked on strengthening viruses that become weak in high temperatures and lose their virulence. The method involved dehydrating the viruses by reducing air pressure and lowering temperature, and our job was developing the machinery to accomplish this.

The water filtration system that Ishii developed in Pingfang was used in Kyoto in the Fushimi district for treating water in saké brewing. The bacteria filter was checked at the army school, and after it passed the checks, it was sent to Manchuria. The checking was done by Naito Ryoichi.

I began working at Pingfang in the spring of 1939. Since Japan is an island country with no borders with other countries, Japanese would be especially susceptible to bacteria and might be expected to succumb readily to pathogens encountered in foreign lands. Although researchers were conducting experiments, many did not think that a bacteriological war could or would really be prosecuted.

Smallpox is endemic to Manchuria, but Manchurians have a degree of natural immunity to the disease. Even without vaccination, the death rate of those afflicted is below thirty percent, while the Japanese death rate was about eighty percent. The disease was epidemic in China and we had to develop a method of preventing it among members of the Japanese army. Test subjects were available in Manchuria. One could see the faces of those scarred by the disease. It was not necessary to use *maruta* for this purpose. *Maruta* were sent in by the *kenpeitai* in Harbin, but we did not have to use them for this disease.

At that time, the general thinking at the unit was that it was necessary to sacrifice three *maruta* in order to save one hundred Japanese soldiers. For a technician though, if a *maruta* is sacrificed without a real reason, it is folly. Technicians have to go into animal cages and work in a dirty environment, but we get accustomed to this. There was much more resistance to going into cells with people.

We worked in the city of Mudanjiang. It is the custom in China that when someone has smallpox a red curtain is hung in the window of the house. When we spotted one of these, we would go in and try to remove and isolate the patient. We used the opium dens as isolation centers, but when we tried taking patients there they would run away. The Manchurians even ran away when we tried to give them preventive vaccinations. With young girls, pock marks on the face mean that they could not be sold at a high price, so parents brought their daughters in for preventive vaccinations. Males were not so concerned with appearance and did not come in to be vaccinated.

We set up a vaccination post at a railroad crossing where the people had to pass every day and forced vaccinations on them. We stamped the hand of each person to identify him or her as having been vaccinated. While the stamp was still wet, some people would transfer the stamp to the hand of a friend who did not want the vaccination. Of course, the character would come out backwards, so we were on the lookout for these. Later, local newspapers carried stories about the smallpox rate having been reduced through our efforts.

In the summer of 1941, five different teams from Unit 731 were dispatched to different areas to treat outbreaks of disease. I was in a unit sent to a town with an outbreak of typhus to treat patients and carry out preventive measures. After that we were called back to Harbin, and then we went to Dalian and boarded a ship. It was not until we were at sea that we were told our destination. We were headed for Saigon. We were conducting water checks in Saigon and just waiting for "X-Day," the opening of war between Japan and the United States. At that time, the water wells in Saigon were under the control and protection of the French army. The Japanese army was very cautious about water supply from experiences in which retreating Chinese had poisoned wells. We kept these thoughts in mind when we moved into Saigon after Japan took over from the French.

In February 1942, Singapore fell to Japan. I was separated from my unit, which went on to Palau, and I was transferred to help set up an Epidemic Prevention and Water Supply Unit branch for the Southern Army in Singapore. I arrived less than one week after Singapore was occupied. The oil tanks were still burning from the battles.

We established the unit at [the former] Raffles Medical University. The unit was set up by Naito Ryoichi and designated Oka 9420 and staffed by about one thousand persons. It was felt that such a large staff was necessary to handle the flow of Japanese personnel going to and coming in from Japan. There were no branch units at outside locations, so when there was an outbreak of disease, teams were dispatched from our unit. The unit leader was Major General Kitagawa Masataka. Within

Unit 9420, disease prevention activities centered around two subunits. One was the Kono Unit, named for that unit's leader and specializing in malaria. I was in charge of the other unit, called the Umeoka Unit. My name was not appropriate for a military unit and so the *Oka* character was borrowed from the main unit's designation, and *Ume* added to form my subunit's name. [The inappropriateness was because the person testifying had an aristocratic name.]

At the time, I was the only civilian subunit leader. My position was equivalent to that of a major. The car at my disposal bore a flag on the fender that was not an officer's flag but was made to look similar, so when I went through the streets soldiers saluted me.

After the Singapore unit was set up in 1942, research into plague was carried on. One stage of this was highly dangerous and handled only by specially trained Japanese staff. But there were also cases of plague infection that occurred within the unit. As far as I know, the dangerous work was not handled by any of the young local boys employed there. Making the vaccine lymph itself was not dangerous, and the local people were enlisted to help in this work. I saw the Singapore *Straits Times* article about a man who worked there when he was a boy. He told of how they chloroformed rats and removed fleas from their bodies. The purpose of that work was to study the percentage of the fleas which are carriers of plague germs and so determine the probabilities of plague epidemics. The purposes for breeding fleas in the laboratory were to develop an antidote against plague and to produce fleas for research.

When the fleas were handled, there was a chance that they could get into people's clothes. So, in that hot climate, people wore loincloths when handling the non-infected fleas. When a flea lands on the bare skin it is immediately discernible and can be brushed off. People wore rubber boots with the tops sealed against their legs with petroleum jelly to prevent fleas from entering.

Singapore was at the front lines of the war and also was the base for the Japanese Southern Army and a supply center, sending materials out to other army units. Prevention of communicable diseases in Singapore was a high priority. The municipal water supply was checked every day, and fresh food supplies were also constantly checked. We performed hygiene checks to a degree never before seen in that area. None of the residents had ever seen such exacting checks carried out. Our activities seemed strange to the local people, soldiers catching rats in the city and bringing them in to have fleas picked from them.

Toward the end of the war, Singapore fell rather early. Malaria was a major cause. The mosquitoes which carry the disease breed in the coral. There were two types of quinine used as preventive medicine; Japan produced a hydrochloride type, and Java produced a sulfate type. The latter was all that was available due to our supplies' being cut off, but it causes severe side effects in the stomach, and for this reason the soldiers refused to take it. This resulted in the malaria's spread. When the American subs started coming into Singapore, the Japanese army was too disabled by sickness to fight them off. Cut off from food and munitions, Singapore fell.

In China, the rat is a deity of happiness. Handling rats the way we did must have appeared foreign to the Chinese. In Manchuria, pneumonic plague became epidemic during the dry season, and we were working on a method of preventing this, but the Manchurians did not realize it.

Naturally occurring epidemics are dependent upon circumstances such as temperature, humidity, and rainfall. Without the concurrence of certain conditions, an epidemic will not occur. Even today, there are certain elements relating to epidemics that are not clear. For example, pickled vegetables depend on the action of microorganisms. Each year produces slightly different results, and even vegetables processed the same year under the same climatic conditions will sometimes vary from one barrel to the next. Artificially induced epidemics, however, are not dependent on such factors.

A case of plague was discovered in Saigon, and I was called there to investigate. Saigon was the base for Japan's advance into Thailand, and the army commanders weighed the question of whether there was a chance of the disease's becoming epidemic. There was a fear that if it happened, goods and equipment could not be unloaded at port. I suggested calling off the advance and was reprimanded, and then I was given time to research the chances of a plague epidemic.

With plague being carried by rats and fleas, the risk of an epidemic is high if three conditions are present: the variety of fleas that carry plague represents a high percentage of the total fleas present on rats; the plague germ is present in those fleas; and the rats carrying the plague-infected fleas are near areas of human activity.

When the rats are put to sleep with chloroform as they were at the Singapore unit, the fleas also are put to sleep. They can then be brushed off onto paper, and the percentage of the plague-carrying variety can be determined. So we went to the harbor and searched the holes that the rats would crawl into. We found that the variety of rat was different and we concluded that there was no chance of plague breaking out.

Back in 1939, at the Nomonhan Incident, the daily variation in temperature was extreme. Japanese soldiers were wearing fur-lined clothing. Gas gangrene bacteria were present on the fur, and if a soldier were hit by a bullet, it would carry the germs into the wound. Gas gangrene takes its name from the fact that when it enters the body it generates a foul-smelling gas. The cause of death of soldiers who died from gas gangrene was not listed as infection but as wounds received in action.

This is a disease that was never seen in Japan. For this reason every day during the battle at Nomonhan, one of the researchers, Ishikawa Tachio, dissected about fifty bodies a day of Japanese soldiers who died from this infection, and he made specimens of about one hundred of them. Whenever lab specimens of humans are mentioned in connection with Unit 731, it is immediately assumed that they were *maruta*. But this was not always the case. There were also specimens made from Japanese casualties.

✳

Lecture, "Unit 731 and Comfort Women" (Nishino Rumiko)

[Nishino Rumiko, who delivered the following lecture, is one of the most active writers and lecturers in Japan on the "comfort women" issue. She has authored numerous books and articles on the subject, and has also involved herself with the story of Unit 731, interviewing numerous former unit members. This lecture was presented at the Unit 731 Exhibition in Takatsuki City, Osaka Prefecture, in December 1994.]

A Korean woman who served in the Japanese military brothels used the Japanese name Haruko. [This was a popular name for non-Japanese women, including comfort women, to adopt.] A Japanese soldier she knew developed a fever, and "Haruko" heard of this and went to take care of him. A personal warmth grew between the two. After that, they were both transferred to Burma, "Haruko" to an army brothel, the soldier to his new duty post. In Burma, the soldier searched for the comfort woman who had helped him, inquiring at the military brothels there, but without success

In 1944, with the war going badly for Japan, the soldier was sent to work at a quarantine station in Harbin. And there fate brought him into a meeting again with "Haruko." It was a brief meeting; the soldier expressed his gratitude with some small gifts, including a fountain pen and some money, and asked for a way to contact "Haruko" in the future. Japan was headed for defeat, and he looked forward to meeting her again after the war.

They never did meet. Then, in recent years the comfort woman problem started surfacing. Survivors among them who suffered shame and stigma for decades have slowly started coming forward, some seeking apology from Japan, others seeking compensation. With all this attention focused on the comfort women of the thirties and forties, the former soldier, now in his eighties, is sending out an appeal to help him search once more for "Haruko."

The former soldier contacted me, and I went to visit him. He told me his story, that he had been a technician and a member of Unit 731 working in the plague research section. But he had another job, giving health examinations to comfort women. Once a week, the women were examined for venereal disease, and he was working in this capacity when he met "Haruko" at the quarantine station in Harbin in 1944.

His work with the comfort women involved taking blood samples from them and sending the samples to Unit 731 for analysis. I have searched out another member of Unit 731 who was also assigned to examining comfort women for venereal disease. He visited the various brothels, at times examining up to one hundred women a day.

Studies of venereal disease were fairly extensive, yet many Japanese books on Unit 731 make no mention of this area. I went into the records of the only court examination of Unit 731 members, the Khabarovsk trials [there were, in fact, trials in China, too], and in the second part of these records was a lengthy record which was released in Japan in the early part of 1950. There was doubt as to its authenticity, but careful corroboration showed it to be true, and within the records it was reported that there was a venereal disease research group within Unit 731. One Japanese writer, Morimura Seiichi, the novelist who has gained a name as a researcher and writer on Unit 731, wrote that venereal disease research was conducted by the tuberculosis research group in Unit 731, under the group leader Futagi. This was supported by the Khabarovsk court records. Morimura was researching former unit members for his writings. He searched out Futagi in Tokyo and found him still healthy, but unwilling to speak on his past work with Unit 731. Futagi later died with his lips sealed.

With the team leader gone, the probe continued, looking for possible survivors among other members of the same team. I searched municipal records and located one man who was then in a hospital in Nagano Prefecture. I traveled there and spoke with him at his bedside. I asked about Unit 731 and he spoke freely about different aspects and activities. Then I asked him about experiments on women. He attitude changed, his lips closed tightly, and he refused to speak further.

I saw that he was fatigued, and since he was over eighty years old, I didn't want to press him in his condition, so I left the hospital. But the subject was on my mind. I decided to go back again the next day. I avoided any mention of experiments on women, and we talked about his postwar life. He told me of how he had come back to Japan, given up his intentions of working as a doctor, and lived secluded in the country, subsisting on the food he grew himself.

I heard his story, thanked him for spending time with me and started to leave the room to return to Tokyo. Just as I reached the door he called to me to wait.

"Last night I thought about our talk," he told me. "I had decided to take this with me to hell, but I thought it over and now I want to leave it in this world." Tears came to his eyes—like a waterfall. Until then he had shown no emotion, but at that moment he changed, and told his story.

He had performed vivisections on six living women. The one experience he did not want to speak of was that concerning a Chinese woman. In vivisections on living persons, sometimes chloroform is used to put the victim to sleep; at times it is not, and the person is cut open fully conscious. This particular Chinese woman, he told me, was put under chloroform but regained consciousness on the table. She started getting up, screaming, "Go ahead and kill me, but please don't kill my child!"

"There were four or five of us working on the vivisection," he told me. "We held her down, applied more anesthesia, and continued."

He told me that he has carried that memory ever since. He felt that bringing it out would place the other surviving members of the team in a difficult position, so for fifty years he had been determined to take that "to hell" with him.

I managed to find one more person who had been a member of the Futagi team for a limited time. He had been a candidate to become a subunit leader under Ishii; he did not get this position but later became Ishii's private driver and assistant. Here is what he told me:

"At first we infected women with syphilis by injection. But this method did not produce real research results. Syphilis is normally transmitted through direct contact. Investigating the course of the disease can offer no useful results unless it is acquired this way. And so we followed a system of direct infection through sexual contact. The reason Unit 731 researched venereal disease was because of the Japanese army's practice of using comfort women. By learning how the disease develops we tried to find a way to protect Japanese soldiers from sexually transmitted disease.

"We were very limited in methods of treating venereal disease at the time, mainly just one type of injection. And a Japanese soldier catching venereal disease would not only be barred from promotion but in some units he would be reduced in rank and placed in detention while he was being treated for it. So, to an army man, catching venereal disease was a disgrace and a setback. As a result, many infected soldiers kept quiet about their infection and tried to get cured secretly. Venereal disease grew into a very serious problem in the military.

"In Siberia, for example, the prices for going to a comfort woman station were prohibitively high compared with the salary of the Japanese soldier. So the soldiers took their pleasures by raping local Russian women. This led to an outbreak of venereal disease, with huge numbers of Japanese soldiers afflicted. The brass at Japanese headquarters saw their soldiers falling to venereal disease, and the problem became grave."

The Marco Polo Bridge Incident and the Rape of Nanjing took place in 1937. There were twenty thousand recorded incidents of rape against Russian women during the period [in the five-month span] between those events alone. With the spread of venereal disease among the ranks and its threat to the discipline and efficiency of the army, it was natural for the high command to look to an army medical unit for a solution to the problem, and Unit 731 was called upon.

Infection of venereal disease by injection was abandoned, and the researchers started forcing the prisoners into sexual acts with each other. Four or five unit members, dressed in white laboratory clothing completely covering the body with only eyes and mouth visible, handled the tests. A male and female, one infected with syphilis, would be brought together in a cell and forced into sex with each other. It was made clear that anyone resisting would be shot. Once the healthy partner was infected, the progress of the disease would be observed closely to determine for example how far it advanced the first week, the second week, and so forth. Instead of merely looking at external signs, such as the condition of the sexual organs, researchers were able to employ live dissection to investigate how different internal organs are affected at different stages of the disease.

The victimization and suffering of women under Unit

731 had not been given much attention in accounts of Unit 731's activities until the comfort women issue was brought to the surface. The focus was largely on a racial basis, how the Chinese and Russians and Koreans were victimized. Now it has become clear how women have suffered as women, and attention is being directed to this issue also.

Another issue being brought closer to the fore now is that of children. Yoshimura Hisato, who later became head of the Kyoto Prefectural University of Medicine, was in charge of frostbite experiments. He was known as an outstanding scholar and researcher. One of his experiments was with a three-month-old baby. A temperature-sensing needle was injected into the baby's hand and the infant was immersed in ice water, then temperature changes were carefully recorded. After the war he issued a paper on this experiment and the results. Since it would have been impossible to conduct an experiment like this in postwar years, it became obvious that this was conducted when he was with Unit 731. From this, we can understand that he used babies born to imprisoned mothers. Records from China identify babies being born to pregnant captives, and also to women made pregnant through forced sex in venereal disease experiments, and these babies were also made use of in the unit's experiments.

One of the former researchers I located told me that one day he had a human experiment scheduled, but there was still time to kill. So he and another unit member took the keys to the cells and opened one that housed a Chinese woman. One of the unit members raped her; the other member took the keys and opened another cell. There was a Chinese woman in there who had been used in a frostbite experiment. She had several fingers missing and her bones were black, with gangrene set in. He was about to rape her anyway, then he saw that her sex organ was festering, with pus oozing to the surface. He gave up the idea, left, and locked the door, then later went on to his experimental work.

❋

Youth Corps member (Anonymous)

[The speaker, seventy-two years old at the time he gave this account, spoke at Morioka City, Iwate Prefecture, in July 1994.]

In 1937, when I was fourteen, they were recruiting for the Naval Air Corps Youth Unit here in Morioka. I stole some money from my father's bureau and went to the recruitment center to join. But there was an army medical officer there, and he called to me and said, "You! Go to the Army Medical College."

I did. In June I entered the Army Medical College in Shinjuku, Tokyo. The officer who told me to go was killed in the Nomonhan Incident in Manchuria.

At school, we were given tough exams, and out of fifty in my class, six or seven were selected. Ishii, the boss, had been to Germany and was our instructor. Afterwards, I was assigned to the Kwantung Army Epidemic Prevention and Water Supply Unit as a civilian employee.

In December, we left the port of Niigata and were taken to Harbin via Korea. I still have an old calling card with my Harbin address. At first we were taken to a Special Service Organization building under the command of an army officer. The first time we were mustered was to hear an address by the unit leader, Ishii. We were the first-year class members of the Youth Corps. The corps was divided into four classes—first-year through fourth-year—of about twenty boys each.

Then we moved to Pingfang and were put through a tough study program. From 8:00 A.M. on, we had courses in such subjects as general education, foreign language, and hygiene. In the afternoon, we assisted the unit members. We worked and studied all the time and had only about three hours' sleep a night. There was a library with extensive stacks of books and foreign language material, and six library specialists to help us.

Before we came to Pingfang, we studied the water filtering device developed by Ishii. We did this at a brick building outside of Harbin and near the medical examination section. We went to Pingfang before the facilities were completed. We were treated well. We were poor, but there in the countryside we had good things to eat that we had never seen before. We had about two years of education under the army, up until July 1939. Next, I was assigned to a team researching bacteria propagation. The others in my class were each assigned to different teams and we didn't see each other very much after that.

We used to go from Pingfang into Harbin to study Chinese. Sometimes we would go to the Unit 731 secret liaison office. I met the boss many times. He treated us with affection. Once when he came into the toilet to bring me toilet paper, he reminded me to "study hard."

I used to call my cap a "chapeaux." I was scolded by the boss several times for that. He would bark at me, "Call it *boshi!*" The army especially disliked foreign terms for nomenclature. [The term was a holdover from the days when the French army was the model for the Japanese army.]

Once, when a few of us boys were walking in the corridor, the boss came up to us and said, "In one year this place used the total tax revenues of Northeast China. That's how important your work is. So work hard." But we were treated with importance only as consumable equipment for war purposes.

At Unit 200, a Unit 731 subunit, we bought three hundred thousand rats for test purposes. I remember the man in charge, Lieutenant Takahashi. He used to be section head of the Iwate Prefectural Hygiene Department [in postwar days].

There were several poison gas test sites outside of Harbin. The Anda site was up against the side of a mountain, and I was there during human experiments. A lot of top brass from the Kwantung Army came to watch. Takeda no Miya was there also. Twenty or thirty *maruta* had their hands tied behind their backs around wooden posts set in the ground, and the gas tanks were on the ground waiting.

For a week before the test, the meteorological team was checking the weather. Then, on one test, the wind shifted and the gas came blowing in our direction, and everybody had to run.

[Takeda no Miya was an imperial prince and a cousin to Emperor Hirohito. It was common practice for people of the imperial family to serve in the military, but Takeda's role in Manchuria is of particular interest. He was the officer in charge of finances for the Kwantung Army, and all money flowing to Manchuria-based units went through his office. He went to Pingfang on numerous occasions and to other units, obviously to check up on how the funds he was dispensing were being spent.

At times he used a pseudonym to conceal his identity. He took one character each from his name and title and reversed them, so that "Takeda no Miya" became "Miyata." A story from another former Youth Corps member recounts the time his unit received a visit from a Colonel Miyata Sanbo. It was midsummer, and it was the custom of the unit administration to place a large column of ice in the rooms of high-ranking guests to bring down the temperature. The Youth Corps boy and his associates all thought it strange that while a colonel was nowhere nearly high enough to receive this courtesy, Miyata's room was honored with an ice column. Later, they discovered the real identity of the man.

By the time of the Tokyo Olympics in 1964, Takeda no Miya was known in Japan as the chairman of the Japan Olympic Committee and vice-chairman of the Tokyo Olympic Organizing Committee. He was also important in other sports circles.]

I remember when I had to deliver the boss's briefcase to the Imperial Household Ministry. [The Imperial Household Agency, known as the Imperial Household Ministry before the war, is a centuries-old organ responsible for all affairs dealing with the emperor and the imperial family. One may assume that tapes being delivered to the ministry were bound for the emperor.] I was attached to the National Hygiene Laboratory then, and I was taken there in an official car with a driver, the unit leader's flag on the fender. I was just this Youth Corps boy, and yet the guard gave me a respectful salute when I handed him the briefcase. It had cans of 16-mm film, probably records of the boss's experiments, and its destination was an imperial conference.

I preserved a lot of human lab specimens in Formalin. Some were heads, others were arms, legs, internal organs, and some were entire bodies. There were large numbers of these jars lined up, even specimens of children and babies. When I first went into that room, I felt sick and couldn't eat for days. But I soon got used to it. Specimens of entire bodies were labeled and identified by nationality, age, sex, and the date and time of death. Names were not identified. There were Chinese, Russians, and Koreans, and also Americans, Britons, and Frenchmen. Specimens could have been dissected at this unit or sent in from other subunits; I couldn't tell.

The glass specimen cases were made by a unit member who had studied glass manufacture in Europe. He made pipettes and all types of glass lab equipment, and he gave me presents of small glass birds he made.

I was given work to do during dissections. I had jobs like carrying buckets full of blood and internal organs. Once, I was allowed to use a scalpel and cut open a *maruta*. I made a long cut from the neck down and cut the body open. It's simple—anyone can do it. After that, the specialists did the fine work.

In order to obtain accurate data from dissection, researchers want to have the *maruta* in as normal a state as possible. Usually they were put to sleep with chloroform, but some were tied down and cut open while fully conscious. At first the *maruta* would let out a hideous scream, but soon the voice would stop. The organs would be removed, conditions such as color and weight would be compared with healthy conditions, and then the organs would be preserved.

One unit team experimented by infecting wheat and watermelon seeds with typhoid and cholera, then cultivating the seeds to determine how the disease was retained in the crops. I heard that the purpose was planting disease-transmitting seeds in enemy territory.

Each of Japan's kamikaze pilots was given a drink of

Imperial saké before leaving on their missions. A Unit 731 member once told me that "that saké is laced with a stimulant that was developed in Unit 731." Afterwards, I heard that the stimulant suppresses fear and agitates the pilots to throw themselves into the attack.

I saw the movie *Black Sun 731* [a Hong Kong production]. In it, the commanding officer bullies the youth squad boys. That was not completely accurate. Research was the first priority. There was harmony among us, and we Youth Corps boys were handled carefully.

At Xinjing I worked with the hygiene team conducting what they called *"manju"* exams. [A *manju* is a bun filled with sweet bean jam; the word is a slang term for a woman's sex organ.] The official name was "disease prevention exams." We went from one brothel to the next, checking the women for syphilis. They had to get on their hands and knees with their buttocks raised for the exam. On a busy day we examined up to one hundred eighty women.

Syphilis would cause a woman's *"manju"* to swell up. Once during an examination, pus discharged from the woman's organ and hit the examiner in the face. A sample of her blood was taken to the unit for analysis and proved syphilitic.

There was an exchange of doctors coming and going from all parts of Japan. Each worked on his own research project and directed it at the unit. One was a former president of the present Iwate Prefectural University Hospital. He came to study bacteriology and became one of the most prominent researchers in Japan in typhoid, cholera, and dysentery. The man who taught me dissection is a leading professor at Kanazawa Medical University.

After I came back to Japan, I worked at making lab specimens.

In the summer of 1940 a plague spread into the capital city of Xinjing. One of the other former Unit 731 members says that it was spread by the unit. I have no way of knowing that, but we were called out and we enclosed the entire affected area in a sheet-metal wall about a meter high, then burned everything inside the enclosure to the ground. Next we examined all the Japanese and Chinese who had lived there. We also secured the areas where the houses had been burned.

The boss ordered us to dig up the bodies of people who had died from the epidemic, dissect them, remove and preserve their organs, and send the specimens back to unit headquarters. In some cases, mobile units came with orders to exhume the bodies and open them up, and then to take small specimens from lungs, livers, and kidneys and apply each to a petri dish. Organs that tested positive for the plague were taken back to the unit. The petri dishes of plague germs we gathered were taken to the Xinjing National Hygiene Laboratory and cultivated, then sent to the boss. That was the most distasteful job I had: violating people's graves.

On many occasions, I saw prisoners taken from their cells wearing leg irons and made to move around the grounds. I think it was around spring of 1939 that I saw three mothers with their children in a test. One was a Chinese woman holding an infant, one was a White Russian woman with a daughter of four or five years of age, and the last was a White Russian woman with a boy of about six or seven.

That was a low-altitude air drop test of typhoid or cholera. The air team and those who knew how to handle bacteria would get into a plane together and spread germs over a village or other areas of population concentration. After that, the area would be examined for the effectiveness of the attack. With plague, fleas were used as a carrier and transported in a ceramic bomb. At first, glass bombs were tried, but they did not work well.

Rats weigh about six hundred grams. They were infected with plague, then they were infested with three thousand to six thousand fleas each and loaded into the ceramic bomb. When the bomb is dropped and breaks, the fleas scatter. But a foolproof method of defense against the bacteria has to be devised, or this cannot be used as a weapon. It's not just the enemy that can be infected, but one's own troops.

The main ingredient of the defoliant used in the Vietnam War was dioxin. Of course, Unit 731 conducted basic research using dioxin. America took those research records and used them.

In the Korean War, doctors who had been in Ishii's unit went there and studied the military effectiveness of dioxin, but nobody speaks about this. They were taken to Korea because America used BW and was unable to protect its own army. That's why the former Ishii unit's men were taken to Korea. I was not there myself and did not see it, but the research in Korea included not just animals but human dissection. I am sure of that.

In Xinjing, I became infected with plague. I don't know how or when it happened, but I ran a high fever and collapsed. I was taken to the air corps hospital at Harbin and treated. The hospital was in a small, separate building from the hospital, and nobody was allowed in without authorization. The doctors were all from Unit 731.

I was sent to Port Arthur, then from there to a hospital in Hiroshima, then to a hospital here in Morioka, then later released. I was infected by the very bacteria we had created, then cured by the serum we had made. I became an unwilling test subject.

I received thirty-six yen a month for medical compensation and continued outpatient treatment. At the time, a school principal was earning eighteen yen a month. The whole family could live on the payments I received. That was hush money. But as a trade-off, a *kenpeitai* officer followed me every day, all day, watching everything I did.

In the hospitals at Hiroshima and Morioka, only the hospital heads knew my sickness. They did not report it to the other doctors. The hospital head at Morioka told me, "It would be best if you did not go back to Ping-fang."

When I was twenty-one, I received an army physical exam and passed. The stamp was put on my paper by the regimental commanding officer, Murakami Yoichi. Below him was the recruiting officer. He came up to me, slapped my face (a normal disciplining method in those days) and asked me where I had been, what I had done, what my background was. I said nothing. Murakami came over and told me, "You don't have to say anything. Go into the navy."

So I went into the navy. During basic training near Yokosuka, we were in bayonet practice when I coughed up blood. The plague was not all out of my system. I was sent to the Yokosuka navy hospital, then to an air force hospital. After that I was transferred to a Red Cross hospital. I studied nursing there while I was being treated, and I learned environmental hygiene. One day, I took a doctor's place on board a minesweeper and we were hit by a torpedo. The ship sank, but I was saved and went to work in the hospital as a hygiene specialist.

Once, in 1960, some of us war buddies had a reunion at a spa in Japan. Among those who had been stationed in Harbin at the time, ninety percent did not know of Unit 731. Thinking of that now, it was idiocy—using people as consumable materials. But at that time I was so involved, I was unaware of reality. In those days, when you said the word *tenno* ["emperor"] and you weren't at attention when the syllable *te* came out, you got your face slapped. This is the first time for me to speak about those days in front of people. My recollection might not be complete, so please forgive me.

One more thing. I cannot give my name yet, but when the time comes, I will identify myself and speak openly about the facts of war, the value of life.

✳

Hygiene specialist (Wano Takeo)

[Wano was attached to Unit 731's Medical Examination and Treatment Center outside of Harbin. He spoke at Morioka City, Iwate Prefecture, in July 1994.]

The Unit 731 examination and treatment center was separated from unit headquarters, so it is less well known. At the time, there were a lot of cases of communicable diseases, and our work was examination, treatment, and prevention of disease for army personnel and their families. The Harbin Army Hospital was inside the city, but our operations were located away from it. We averaged about seventy patients per day.

Our building was called the south wing, a wooden

structure built by Unit 731. Next door was a brick building, and I saw the Ishii water purification machine in there. When I went there, the building was not finished yet and I was assigned to Pingfang for a while.

In our work, the biggest fear was the danger of getting infected ourselves, with plague and other diseases. When a plague patient came in everyone was so careful of cuts that we avoided shaving.

My main work was examining blood, urine, and feces, and looking for changes in hemoglobin. During the four years I was at the south wing I made frequent visits to the headquarters at Pingfang. I also had to go into the prisons to deliver the blood samples that I brought from our division, and receive blood samples and tissue specimens.

When we entered the prison buildings, we had to walk through a tray of disinfectant. Then we were inspected at a door, and finally met the person we were to hand the samples to. Miyamoto, the man who worked there, later died of typhoid. I used to meet him and a technician there all the time; I never met them outside of that room.

The blood samples I received from them were taken from *maruta* who were infected with viruses. The samples were in prepared slides. I traveled by truck between Pingfang and the south wing twice a day, carrying specimens and papers. Another part of my job was carrying human organs.

There was no real research in vaccine at the examination and treatment division. The Pingfang teams developed an invigorative solution, and we injected it into patients who were close to recovery. The base was garlic, and I injected it into myself sometimes to overcome fatigue.

We used a lot of Chinese workers. Some couldn't work without heroin, and we gave it to them.

At the south wing we also performed dissection. One of the researchers had dissected a huge number of *maruta* at Pingfang and came to be known as the "dissection wizard." He's now active in the medical world.

We had a patient at the south wing who was a member of Unit 731. I thought that he had contracted syphilis, but he had the plague, and he died. I think his body was sent to Pingfang. And people who died at the south wing were all dissected. If no family member came we would dissect immediately and preserve them. The preserved bodies were probably sent to Pingfang.

There were nutrition specialists at south wing, and they were consulted by Pingfang for advice on diets for the *maruta*.

An order came from Unit 731 to form examination and treatment teams, and go out into the villages to treat the people. An unknown disease broke out among one of the tribes and we went out there. It was typhus, and we treated it for fifteen days, then came back. Another time we went out to a town between Harbin and Xinjing when typhoid broke out. Our job was to keep it from spreading.

Unit 731 was working to make biological weapons. For that, it is also necessary to have a knowledge of treatment of disease. Our division went to treat people, but our work required the dissection of *maruta*. Our data was used in the development of biological weapons, and the total direction of all our efforts was toward warfare.

On August 10, 1945, we boarded a train at Harbin. We heard talk about an uprising in Korea, but in about ten days we made it back to Japan.

There is one thing I would like to mention about this exhibit. It is stated that when the war ended, rats ran around infecting people with plague. That is not true. I heard that the rats were all killed with chemicals and did not infect the area. The *maruta* were also killed.

✳

Hygiene specialist (Anonymous)

[The speaker gave this talk at Morioka City, Iwate Prefecture, in July 1994.]

Five people were selected from each prefecture to become hygiene specialists, and I was one of Iwate's five. In January 1941, we arrived in Dalian. We spent three months training in a unit there, and in March I was transferred to Pingfang and entered Unit 731. I was eighteen years old.

At the former unit we were always hit around by the senior soldiers, and it was rough. But at Unit 731, there was harmony. There were only medical officers and civilian doctors. There was no seniority among soldiers, no noncommissioned officers. The facilities and the food were good, and we didn't get hit.

As soon as we came to Unit 731, I heard rumors about human experiments. They told us, "You're in a unit that infects prisoners with bacteria and dissects them. Get yourself ready for it."

From April to July, we had general education. There were about two hundred of us in the same residence hall. Later, we worked at dissecting dogs. After I opened up a dog, the instructor explained the organs.

Part of our work was growing bacteria in glass dishes.

They warned us not to touch the bacteria with our hands. We were told, "Don't remove the cover until you get the order to do so." We were ordered to apply the bacteria culture medium to the glass dish as a preparation stage and leave it overnight. In twenty-four hours, the bacteria would generate. The medium was sweet, like jelly, and we would eat it. The officer would scream at us, "If you eat that, you'll die."

During the education period, we followed orders. They told us, "Always keep your gas mask with you." Sometimes we could go into town for the night. They'd take us in a truck, we'd go to the movies and have fun in town, then the truck would pick us up again and take us back to the unit.

Ishii, the unit leader, was an exalted man—he was higher than the emperor. I thought that he was a great man because of the water filtration system he had invented. I almost cried from appreciation.

Sometimes I drove truckloads of Chinese for tests. Around May 1941—we were still wearing winter uniforms—we were told to load some Chinese prisoners into a truck. There was just a mat rush on the floor of the truck. We had guns, but I don't think they were loaded. The newest members of our group had less than half a year of service.

The officers told us where to take the Chinese. We pulled the canopy over the back of the truck and started out. There were between twenty and thirty of them. We drove for about three or four hours and we were told to stop and unload the Chinese. We were in an open plain; there was nothing around. The interpreter told the Chinese, "Go!" and they were happy to be running around. They were all men, all built better than we were, some in good clothing with shoes, others in sandals. Some were coal carriers, still black with coal dust the way they had been when they were picked up. Others were dirty with the soil of whatever work they were doing.

The truck went back empty. A couple of civilian employees and four or five soldiers stayed. A few days later, I carried another load of about the same number of people out there to the same place. The ones we had brought before were still there, lying huddled together on the ground in groups of five or six, blue with cold, begging, "Help . . . help." So we carried them by hand back to the truck. When we got back to the unit, we were ordered back to the barracks. That was the only time I ever carried anyone in such bad shape, but I made three or four trips out to the plain carrying prisoners. They were strong and healthy when we hauled them out there, but later they were shaking, screaming: "My stomach hurts!"; "I'm finished!": "I'm dying!"

I didn't know whether they had been infected by our bacteria or what. I wasn't even sure if they were prisoners. I had not yet heard that word *maruta*. When were drinking saké together with the officers we asked about those Chinese. We were told, "That's not for you to ask!"

The third time I brought a load of Chinese out to the plain, there were two or three trucks that were returning empty stopped by the side of the road. I pulled my truck over, and there was an old man sitting there on a mat rush holding a skylark. I started up the truck again and heard some gunshots. I stopped and looked back, and the old man was lying dead. Later, I asked a researcher about it. He told me, "Don't ever say a word about that. He was a spy."

There was an airfield near the unit headquarters. There were lots of planes, and when they took off in the morning it was noisy. Planes from other units used to land there often. I was once told that a plane that had just left had gone for a plague germ attack on the Chinese army. But a civilian researcher told us, "The bacteria that you fellows cultivated were spread in Nanjing, or somewhere in China." Once, someone said that the bacteria that we made had been cultivated well, and four or five Chinese had died. We cheered ourselves. "We're medal earners," we said. We were really proud.

There was a big smokestack in the unit. On some days it poured smoke, sometimes there was none. It was far from our barracks. Once, we asked what was burning. The answer was "prisoners."

The building with the stack was near the barracks for the education officers. One day when I walked by there, the wives of the officers were polishing brass objects that looked like trophies. Someone told me, "Those are bombs."

Afterward, I asked a civilian researcher about them. He told me, "The bacteria that you fellows made were loaded into those and dropped for dispersal. Maybe in Chongqing, or Shanghai." That was around June 1941.

I watched the wives polishing the bombs in the corridor of the building. Then I noticed, farther inside at a wide space in the corridor, there was a human specimen in a jar. The jar was the size of a person, and what looked like a young Russian soldier was preserved inside in liquid. His body was cut in half, lengthwise. I realized later that it was a White Russian.

There were other specimen jars there, also, but they were all covered over with cloths, and I couldn't see what was inside. I figured that perhaps the Russian specimen should have been covered, too, and someone had removed the cover.

Just then, an officer saw me, screamed, "That's forbidden!" and I ran out. That evening, the officer in charge of our barracks said to us, "The person who saw the preserved Russian specimen, raise your hand." Nobody raised a hand. He got angry and ordered us to slap each other's faces. "All right," he said. "That was self-punishment. Now tell me truthfully, who saw the Russian specimen?" I thought it was all right now, so I raised my hand. Then the officer hit me on the head with a kendo fencing stave.

The Special Forces men had taken a lot of photos. They were big: bodies with no heads, with no feet, with swollen bellies. That was from water torture. They force water into the body to swell up the belly. My buddy Mikami told me, "I saw the whole thing. It was really hideous." I told him, "That's war." I killed people for the country—for the emperor. That was my belief then.

In August 1941, we got on a train to be transferred, but I didn't know where we were headed. When we got to Harbin, the officer in charge told us we were going to Hailar. After four or five days on the train, we arrived near the Russian border. A truck met us at the station. There were members of all different teams and units among us. We were ordered, "Epidemic Prevention and Water Supply Unit members, take one step forward." They split our group up, and I was in the group sent to Unit 543. That was a branch unit of Unit 731 in Hailar. I was stationed there for three years, until 1944. Our barracks was right in front of the station, an old Russian barracks, and I remember hearing the trains coming and going during the night.

We conducted field tests of water quality. We were supposed to work through October, until the cold weather sets in, but actually we worked in the winter also. We loaded tents, charcoal, vessels, and other equipment into two trucks and took off with a team of about fifteen people. There were army doctors, hygiene specialists, and noncommissioned officers.

We drove up near the Nomonhan region. We drew water samples into test tubes and labeled them with the place, date, and time of sampling, and a code. When we found rivers frozen, we had to break through the ice to get samples. We drove around taking samples like that for about one or two weeks at a time. Sometimes we stayed over at another unit and could get a hot bath.

At one place, an army doctor pulled out a test tube with a kind of bacteria that looked something like mold, added water, shook it, and threw it into a sample of water we had taken from a well. I saw that happen two or three times. Later, we tested the water and took photos. Water sampling is a simple way to describe our work, but actually we were field tacticians.

There was a Mongolian settlement we came to. They were all happy to see us, and the little girls picked flowers for presents. We exchanged things with them for dried fish and meat. We conducted field strategy there two or three times, then everyone in the settlement suffered from diarrhea and came down with sickness. The last time we went there, they didn't bring flowers and they didn't want anything of ours. Our interpreter told us that they said we had thrown something into the well and made everyone sick. Our officer in command joked about it and told the Mongolians, "You're the ones who threw it into the well."

I had some creosote and gave it to the Mongolians. They were glad to get it. The officer saw that and told me not to give them any medicine, but he didn't press the issue any further. He just said, "Better stay away from them," and later he told us never to go back there again.

One of our members drank that well water by mistake. He had been near the Mongolian settlement, he was thirsty, and his canteen was empty. The army doctor had told us not to drink any water except what was in our canteens. The soldier said that the well water was all right, why not drink it? The answer was, "Never mind. Just don't drink it."

But he did drink it, and when the officer heard that he screamed, "You're going to die!" The soldier said, "But I don't feel sick."

I found out later about our team throwing bacteria into the well. I don't know what happened to that soldier after that.

Around 1942, I came to realize that what we were doing was not field tactics, but biological warfare. But not everything that we did was bad. The Hailar unit treated illness in some villages, giving injections.

In the autumn of 1943, Warrant Officer Murakami committed suicide. He had come to Manchuria with his young wife. He had thrown bacteria into the water supply near a Special Forces detachment, and several people drank that water and died. Strong words came from the Special Forces officers. Why did he throw that into the water? The main work of the unit was supposed to be water sampling. Maybe when people came up and accused us of making them sick, it was too much for him.

A few days after that, the fellow who always worked with Murakami, Sergeant Maruyama, committed suicide. Maybe he was under pressure from the officers.

He had killed himself in an army comfort woman

brothel. And it was an officers' brothel. This was a big problem for the army, and I was ordered to go get the body before news leaked out.

At the time, there were three classes of brothels. Class 1 was for officers, Class 2 was for noncoms, and Class 3 was for civilian employees and enlisted men. But even those who were not officers had a chance to go to the Class 1 brothels. Units were given certain days on which their men could use the officers' brothel. On days when we had no duty and would be going to the brothel, we would muster in the morning at 8:30. They would inspect our condoms, and anyone with a condom with a hole in it would not be allowed off base. Enlisted men were allowed off base from 8:30 until supper time. We used to line up at the brothel and wait our turn. We would each be finished in ten to fifteen minutes. Noncoms could stay out until 10 P.M., and officers until the following morning.

The brothels were under civilian management, but some were for the exclusive use of army personnel. There were almost no Chinese women in them; almost all were Koreans. The medical unit of the Twenty-third division used to go in there to perform VD checks, and they issued health certificates.

There were also brothels for civilian employees of Japanese corporations like Shimizu and Kajima construction companies, but venereal disease was more rampant among civilians.

I went to the brothel to get the body. Maruyama had taken potassium cyanide, and a Korean comfort woman was crying in the room. The Japanese manager of the brothel was angry at the commotion caused by the man's suicide. I calmed him down with a few small presents, then I wrapped the body in a blanket and brought it back to the unit. One of the sergeants cremated the body and sent the ashes to Maruyama's home town.

We were ordered out. On the way to the station an officer told us, "You fellows will be headed southward. So I now cut all connection with the Epidemic Prevention and Water Supply Unit. You have no reason to feel guilty about anything, so go fight proudly."

We were a disease prevention unit, so we were issued only small arms. On the way, I had a barber take clippings of my hair and nails and send them to my home.

We crossed Korea to Pusan and boarded a ship. En route, we were hit by a torpedo from an American submarine. About two thousand men were killed. We survivors were transferred to another ship, and we headed for Shanghai. Again, we got hit by an American torpedo. I escaped death again. About eighty percent of those on board went down. The ship rolled over, and I could hear the men trapped inside calling out, "*Tenno heika banzai!*" ["Eternal life to His Imperial Majesty"] Others cried, "Mother!"

Finally, we docked in Taiwan and took on medical supplies. We were supposed to head for Mindanao but ended up landing in the Philippines in December 1944. We were sent to a field hospital bringing medical supplies to a station in the mountains. In early January, we were shelled by a warship.

From there, we had combat against the Americans. That was rough. Nothing in Unit 731 was even a fraction that bad. The war ended, and we knew nothing about it. In January 1946, a plane flew over and dropped leaflets to inform us that the war was over. They carried pictures of General MacArthur and General Yamashita shaking hands. One day, my buddies and I had laid our guns under a tree and were eating apricots when a Japanese and an American officer came and said, "Let's go back to Japan together." I was ready to keep fighting, but I gave in and was taken prisoner. Later we were taken back to Japan, and I landed at Nagoya.

One reason I came to this Unit 731 Exhibition was to see if I might contact other former members. I spoke with one man who had lost his sight in an American bombing attack. He died recently and until the end he did not want to meet with other former members.

Another man that I located and contacted by phone laughed, "That was fifty years ago." That's about all he would say.

I was never ordered not to speak about the unit, or not to contact other members. So, wherever I go, I speak about it, and search for others who were there. Ishii wouldn't believe it. But he did give that order and if he had lived to see it, he wouldn't have allowed it.

When I first entered Unit 731, I had no idea that it was that kind of unit. I thought it was to help the people of China by providing clean water. The Japanese enjoy drinking good water, so I naturally thought that water supply would be our job. When I came to the Unit 731 Exhibition the first time, I was shocked. I had heard rumors, but I never even knew the word "*maruta.*" I had heard rumors about the dissections, and I wondered if those things really happened. I thought that if they had really happened, they were wretched acts. But, personally, I feel no shame. I thought that I was really doing a good thing.

✳

Kenpeitai member (Iwasaki Ken'ichi)

[The water torture was used for the fifteen years that Japan spread its "coprosperity" through China. Former kenpeitai *member Iwasaki has appeared many times before audiences to tell of the role his organization played in supporting the occupation and supplying victims for human experiments. The water torture was used mainly to force confessions from those who resisted the Japanese invasion and occupation, and a replica of the water torture system was built for the travelling exhibit.]*

There were special tables such as the one at the exhibition built for this purpose, but sometimes an ordinary bench or a ladder was used. I first saw this device when I was assigned to the Harbin branch. I thought it was a very handy system and was delighted with it. I used it for six years, until the end of the war. Yet many officials who participated in the invasion never saw one, and even some *kenpeitai* officers are seeing it for the first time at these exhibits.

The victim is placed naked on the board face up. The head is held immobile inside a wooden box frame fixed at the end of the board. The arms and legs are strapped down. The victim is not able to move no matter how great the suffering. If a hose is used to force water into the mouth, as had been the case previously, the victim can evade some of the water. A different system was devised, an easier one whose results are more complete.

First, water is poured on the chest to prevent a heart attack. A cloth is placed over the mouth and nose, and water is trickled over it slowly. The cloth becomes saturated, and no matter how much the victim tries to fight, water enters the body and in five or six minutes the belly swells. This is continued until the desired confession is obtained. The reason for devising this system was that it was easy to use and did not leave any visible scars as evidence of torture.

Concerning the human experiments, I had some idea that they were going on but it was secret and we were not informed. Sometimes people would not confess under any amount of torture. Their bodies would be broken down but they would not give in. If we released them, they would accuse us of torturing them, so we sent them to the Ishii unit.

Condemned prisoners from all over were brought to us at Harbin. Instead of being executed, they were used for freezing experiments in Harbin's subzero winters. I knew that these tests were necessary if we were going to have to fight Russia.

There were occasional parties to commemorate someone's work. A committee would decide on carrying out executions while everyone was drinking saké. There was one officer who was especially fond of executions. He would have about five persons sit in front of a ditch, then behead them and kick the bodies into the ditch. These particular executions apparently had no scientific aims.

I thought it was good that the place was blown up after the war and the secrets did not get into the hands of the Russians. Everyone else thought so, too.

✳

Three Youth Corps members (Anonymous)

[These men held a panel discussion at the Iwate exhibition site. All three still retain anonymity, and are listed here simply as Y-san, T-san and K-san.

Y-san and T-san were in a group that was sent to Manchuria as

Japan was on the verge of collapse. The war ended without their knowing the real function of Unit 731. When the outfit was getting ready to pull out from its base, T-san was given the job of disposing of the maruta.

Some time after the war, K-san formed a group with other former Unit 731 members. Some former unit members are planning a trip to China to apologize to surviving family members. K-san remarks on this by quoting a Buddhist teaching: "'The Buddha is never far away; he is always near.' It isn't necessary to go to China; visiting Tama Cemetery is all right."]

K-SAN: We were the Youth Corps; that is, we were transferred into a special environment. So when talk started in the postwar years about forming our association, there were voices against it. In 1953, we held a large Buddhist memorial service with some former Unit 731 members, including those who were active in the headquarters under Ishii and Kitano. We later formed a Memorial Service Association and have kept the group going ever since. We published a newsletter, and it has now reached more than one hundred issues.

In 1955, our association erected a cenotaph in the Tama Cemetery in Tokyo and held a memorial service to console the spirits of the sacrificed *maruta*. Since then, we have held a service every year on the first Sunday following August 15, and this has gradually brought the existence of Unit 731 out before the public. But this is only a once-a-year event.

Then, in 1993, we held a large meeting of members from all over Japan. We plan to hold more, sending out the word for any former Unit 731 people to come together and join us.

T-SAN: When I was in elementary school, a former student of our school about six years senior to us came flying over in a trainer and dropped a message in the schoolyard. It read, "Underclassmen! Come and follow us!" That got us enthusiastic about joining the Youth Corps of the armed services. Then we were told that if we came to Unit 731 we would get to ride in planes. I was excited by airplanes, so I applied. Our school had a three-month-long "Manchuria and Mongolia Development Volunteer Corps" educational program, and after finishing that we were sent over to China. We were fifteen and sixteen years old, the youngest in our town to go overseas.

We rode a night train for Niigata, our port of embarkation. When we reached the harbor, there were reports of American submarine activity in the Japan Sea and our ship was kept in port for one week. It would have been all right if we had left right away, but the waiting got to us. The boys lost interest in going and a lot of them became cranky and cried. The education officer hit the criers with the scabbard of his sword and screamed, "Don't cry!"

Y-SAN: I applied for the air corps also. We were mustered at Morioka University.

T-SAN: But the name of the unit was not 731—it was 731-T. That's because it was a secret unit. That got us angry when we found out.

Y-SAN: When I got to Unit 731, I thought it strange that on Mondays and Fridays smoke always poured from the big chimney. One day, I was out on the farm where the unit grew vegetables to maintain self-sufficiency in food. The officer in charge of raising crops was there.

"They're burning again today," he said to me.

"Burning what?" I asked.

"Logs."

"But if there are no trees around, how come there are logs to burn?" I wondered.

Then he leveled with me and told me that it was corpses that were making the smoke. He added, "They're spies." In my fourteen-year-old innocence, I thought, "Ah! They were bad people."

T-SAN: In June 1945, we celebrated the anniversary of the founding of Unit 731. We were given special treats to eat.

K-SAN: That was a critical point in time for Unit 731. People were asking what would happen to the unit. Japan had a nonaggression pact with Russia, but that was a treaty made to be broken. The question was, When would they attack? Unit 731 was researching for war against the Soviets.

Unit 731 was not a combat unit. That meant that in the event of an attack, we would have to evacuate and run. The biggest problem would be destroying the evidence.

From May 1945, the lights in the office of the unit leader's office were burning bright. I knew then that something must be happening, but I was too low down in rank to be told what. I found out later that there were conferences of officers going on, and that things were getting bad.

As I mentioned, the point that was constantly under discussion was whether the Soviets would attack or not. And if so, when. Ishii was very democratic. He asked me, an absolute lowest ranking member of the unit, and in polite terms of address that one would normally direct to a person of importance, "What are your thoughts on the matter? Will they attack, or not?"

I answered, "They will."

"And when will it be?"

"After the harvest," I answered.

The educational officer was Lieutenant Colonel Nishi. He was in charge of another branch unit. He felt differently. "That's not correct," he said. "According to my information, they will not attack."

Ishii listened, then ordered Nishi to go to his unit, near the Russian border, and investigate. He never returned. He was captured by the Russians, put on trial at Khabarovsk, and sentenced to twenty-five years at hard labor.

Then it happened. The Soviets came into the war against Japan on August 9. Our unit had military men, civilians, and family members. We were issued small bottles of potassium cyanide to take if we were captured. Ishii was asked what steps were to be taken with the families.

"Let them commit suicide too," was the answer. Major General Kikuike spoke up against that, saying that "we're military men. We're ready to die at any time. But it isn't right for us to kill family members. The unit should take care of getting the families back to the mainland."

The Examination and Treatment Unit was inside the Pingfang compound. Those who could not kill themselves could go there and have it done for them. [In the end, the families were evacuated.]

Y-SAN: I was on security patrol at Togo Village after the families left. The Manchurians would come to steal things, and I was on guard. I also had to burn the remaining corpses. The team leader led us into the cells, and we pulled the corpses out and incinerated them. Then we disposed of the bones. There was a place where animal bones from meals were thrown, and we loaded the *maruta* bones into a truck and threw them into the same garbage dump. Those *maruta* had been killed by gas. When our team got to the cell blocks, the bodies were already pulled outside. We had to pour fuel oil on the bodies to keep them burning, because they kept piling up.

K-SAN: We started a new activity in our association. When people see the Unit 731 Exhibition, they think that the unit itself was evil and criticize it. That also contains some error. Our work now should be to leave the truth of history to the people of the future. We want to cooperate with people like Professor Tsuneishi and with groups researching this period. If scholars are going to make judgments, they need research materials, and we have the materials to offer. To make a flat judgment of equating Unit 731 with evil is unwise. So we decided to join with scholars and conduct academic surveys and research.

I first met Ishii Shiro in 1958, on August 17. He said that Unit 731 was an organization that was formed to save Japan, and that when the outfit's time came, it would be announced openly to the world. "You former unit members had no way to apologize," he said, and he bowed his head deeply. Unit 731 conducted research that was unique in the world, and it should be left to the world. On the other hand, there are various ways of thinking in our group. Ishii ordered his men to take the secret to the grave with them, didn't he?

T-SAN: Right. That's what we were told.

K-SAN: I had left for the battlefront, and I didn't hear it myself, so I was in a state of innocence. But I found out much later, in 1958, from Ishii directly. I thought it was time to be released from any obligation of silence. We were free from the muzzling order. Our

Memorial Service Association had been formed three years earlier. But is anyone really living in hiding from his past as a member of 731? T-san, you were in the unit for only three or four months. Did you feel it was wrong to come out and reveal it?

T-SAN: No, I didn't feel that.

Y-SAN: There is still a problem of being told that it's wrong for any of us to talk about what we're carrying inside. It was only in 1991 that I made contact with three former Unit 731 men. After the war, I came home a soldier, wearing my army uniform. Then I received one thousand yen. Others, I heard, received three hundred and five hundred yen. That was hush money.

K-SAN: That was not hush money. The money was brought by an army officer. There were still Unit 731 members in Manchuria. That was salary, not hush money.

[This an area of disagreement among former members. Other reports of hush money, however, are convincing, since many payments of huge amounts were made two to three years after the war.]

K-SAN: The Youth Corps made Anda airfield. It was in a remote area that had dry fields with a high alkali content, so there were lots of weeds, and the soil was no good for crops. Unit 731 found that place and made it into an airfield. More than one hundred Youth Corps boys worked on it, leveling the ground with shovels. But first we had to burn the dry grass. That was a scary job. The fire flared up wild. Even the officer in charge was frightened. He screamed, "Put it out! Put it out!" A hot wind came blowing at us and burned our eyebrows. When we thought we had the fire under control, it would flare up in another place and come at us again. The Manchurians in the area had to run.

K-SAN: We were issued potassium cyanide by the team leader. That's why Unit 731 members were suspect when the Teigin Incident happened. The potassium cyanide was given to everyone. Maybe some fourteen-year-olds would have drunk it if they'd been captured by the Russians. That's what education does. We had to give the poison back after we reached Japan.

When we pulled out of Pingfang we were armed, so we were able to reach Pusan. On the way, we were attacked by Koreans.

T-SAN: After we'd burned the bodies, our next job was to destroy the prison cells. We chiseled holes in the wall, about as big around as your thumb, and the explosives experts planted dynamite. But it wouldn't break the walls down. Those facilities were built strong. Even the windows were tough to break.

Unit 731 had planes called *Donru* ["Big Dragon."] that were very effective in the war. They could launch torpedoes and flare shells, and they broke down the buildings with aerial torpedoes. At the time, the tallest building in Japan was the Marunouchi Building. The Pingfang building was several times higher. And the facilities were the best. There was a good boiler and heating system because of the cold winters.

K-SAN: I remember the night they woke us and ordered us to destroy the buildings and equipment. I had to go in to clean out the cells and there were pillows in there that were all bloody. Ordinary pillows, several of them in one room. That puzzled me.

It took us three days to destroy the facilities. We

probably started on the tenth of August, because the Soviets came into Manchuria on the ninth. My elder sister was working on the army telephone switchboard in Xinjing. She called me and said that we'd be going home. I think that was before we started breaking up the buildings, and before the Soviets came into the war. It might have been around the seventh or eighth that she called and told me that.

Y-SAN: I think the first time I saw Ishii was when we were getting ready to destroy the buildings. We were all mustered, getting orders from the officers. I was all the way in the back, and Ishii was sitting up front, so all I saw was the back of his head. In fact, I don't really know if it was Ishii.

When we left Pingfang, we all loaded onto a train and pulled out. There were food supplies already on board, and we traveled day and night. When we got to Changchun, the train engineer ran away and we sat there for two or three days until a replacement could be found. They had to bring him at gunpoint.

[The problem of the fleeing engineer is mentioned also by Akama Masako, who was evacuated on the same train. This is clarified by a Chinese historical researcher who came to Japan to attend the Iwate exhibition.]

Y-SAN: At the end of the war, Unit 731 members raced for the Korean border. Lines of communications were jammed, and confusion was everywhere. When the train got to Changchun it was known that the war was over. At least the leaders and the train engineer knew, and that's why the engineer fled. He was Chinese, and if he were to enter Korea he would be in trouble.

The officer in charge distributed potassium cyanide

in small brown bottles, telling us, "If you're captured, drink this." The bottles were confiscated later, after we left Manchuria and the leaders felt that we had made good our escape from the Russians. Then, when we landed in Japan, we were told, "Don't contact other members of the unit. Say nothing to anyone about it."

I was there only three to four months, so there are many people who I wouldn't know. And we have nothing left from those days. They made us burn everything, even photos of our families that we had carried with us. So we don't remember names or faces.

❋

Nurse attached to Unit 731 (Akama Masako)

[Akama went to Unit 731 as a nurse attached to the maternity section. Her husband and uncle were also in the unit, and her cousin worked in the boiler room, making four family members connected with 731.

She went back to China in recent years to apologize for the deeds of Unit 731. She met with the wife of a man who had been tortured and then sent to Unit 731, where he was sacrificed in the experiments. His name was found in old municipal records, and his crime was listed as transmitting anti-occupation information by wireless radio.

At her appearance before some one thousand people in Takatsuki, Osaka Prefecture, Akama spoke with difficulty, the result of advanced age and poor physical condition. She advised her listeners that this was the last time she would appear before an audience.]

With the syphilitic mothers, the doctor in charge of our team delivered the *maruta* babies himself instead of having the nurses do it, as would normally be the case. At that time, he would order me to stop the blood flow from the mother to the baby. The doctor would take a sample of the blood, then I would let small quantities of blood flow intermittently, as he took successive samples. The test tubes were all lined up on the shelf. He was checking to determine the intensity of the syphilis transmitted from mother to child, and the progression of the disease from the time of birth.

A researcher came running in, screaming that some *maruta* had escaped. They were caught by the Special Forces. That was the team under Ishii Shiro's brother, Ishii Takeo. Only someone who could be trusted was admitted to that team. They shot the escapees.

When it came time to evacuate, we got into a train and left the unit headquarters. It was a long train, maybe twenty or thirty cars. A soldier came running to me and said that a baby was going to be born in a freight car at the end of the train. We ran back through the cars. The wife of one of the unit members was there in labor, and there were soldiers with lots of medals. Surrounded by those high-ranking officers, I delivered the baby. That was August 15, 1945. We were passing through Xinjing. The train engineer ran away, and we couldn't move. Planes were flying overhead, keeping lookout; soldiers were around us. I was trembling in fear. This, I felt, was really war.

Then, we heard the emperor's words ending the war. We were always told to "work hard and Japan will definitely win." When I heard that we had lost, I was sad.

It grew dark. Ishii came over to us carrying a big

candle and said, "I'm sending you all back home. When you get there, if any one of you gives away the secret of Unit 731, I personally will find you, even if I have to part the roots of the grasses to do it." He had a fearful, diabolical look on his face. My legs were shaking. And not just at me—at everyone. "Even if I have to part the grasses . . ."

He told us never to go for a job in a public office. That order limited my husband's chances of employment in Japan. He couldn't apply for a job with a government agency, and he ended his life doing hard work. He wasn't made for that.

❈

Kenpeitai officer (Naganuma Setsuji)

[Naganuma was eighty-one years old at the time he gave this talk. He spoke at Takatsuki City, Osaka Prefecture, in December 1994.]

I am a war criminal. I served in Manzhouguo [Manchukuo], that phony country created by Japan.

In August 1945, the Soviets invaded Manchuria. I was captured and imprisoned for five years in the Soviet Union, where I did forced labor on very meager rations. I was in my early thirties and still strong, so I managed to survive. A lot of those in their fifties and sixties died of malnutrition and exhaustion. There were too many prisoners for the Russians to handle—some six hundred thousand. They returned most of the prisoners to Japan and kept about one thousand of us considered to be war criminals.

Then we were sent to China and placed in a big prison

that had been built by the Japanese army. We spent six years there, undergoing mental training— brainwashing.

When I was doing my work in Manchuria, I arrested a spy. He was a Korean who had taken part in his country's independence movement, then gone to the Soviet Union for education. He had come to Dalian through the headquarters of the Chinese Communist Party and was a bright and efficient spy. He observed the movements of Japanese army baggage and equipment and other details of troop activity, and sent the information to the Soviet Union by wireless radio.

Then we found a connection to the Soviet consulate in Dalian. I was in charge of the squad that attacked the place. I took about sixty men, and we surrounded the consulate. We arrested everyone in the spy ring and found one wireless transmitter. We also found the names of spies in other cities, and they were arrested, too.

I received orders from my unit commander to send four of the arrested men to Unit 731. At that time I had no sense that I was a party to any killing. I only filed the papers and sent the men to Unit 731.

In 1992, a group of us former *kenpeitai* men went to China to apologize to the family members of the people we had sent to Unit 731. One woman, now about sixty, was the grandchild of one of the victims. She told us, "Our grandfather was killed by Unit 731 in experiments. He was killed because the *kenpeitai* sent him. If you hadn't sent him, he would have lived. You are killers just like those doctors." We prostrated ourselves in apology, and she kept pressing the fact home that we were partners in the crime—as guilty as the doctors of Unit 731.

And it's true! It is just as she said. Apologizing does not erase the crime. After I got out of prison in China, I spoke with my fellow former *kenpeitai* members. We were the aggressors. Most of the Japanese participants in the war were aggressors. Orders came from above—orders from the emperor—and people were killed because it couldn't be helped. According to international convention, those who kill in combat are not criminals. The three thousand people killed by Unit 731 were all sent there by the *kenpeitai* or the police. We thought we were doing good for the army by sending prisoners there. From the point of view of the families of the victims, even killing the *kenpeitai* would not be satisfaction enough, and I represent one of those *kenpeitai*.

When this Unit 731 Exhibition brought out testimonies like my own, many people were cynical and asked why we were silent for so long. People come to these exhibitions and say, "I was in the Youth Corps then," and "I was doing this or that then." The pioneering group who went to develop Manchuria sometimes tell how they cooperated with Unit 731 without knowing, by providing rats for experiments, and they also say "We were accessories to the crime." My younger brother told me there's no need to talk about those days now. He told me to forget it, to be quiet about it. I became chairman of our senior citizens club, and I was told the same thing there. There's no use in talking about those things now. Forget it.

An honorary professor at Ibaraki University wrote in a newspaper article, "'The Japanese army committed all sorts of cruelties in China and Southeast Asia. Japanese children know nothing about it. Why? Because the parents say nothing about it."

I also said nothing. These days, there are all sorts of moves toward friendship with China and Asian nations— but without children's knowing these things it is impossible to establish real friendship. It is the duty of those who experienced war to tell these things to their children and grandchildren, to tell of the real horrors of war.

When I read that statement, it strengthened my resolve to speak out. Unit 731 is being written about in Japanese books now. People like Dr. Yamaguchi are studying it from a medical point of view, asking how it could have happened. But these are all peripheral issues. The main point is that the objective of Unit 731's work was the development of bacteriological weapons. The situation with Japan grew worse, and Ishii and the army knew that Japan was losing and Russia would attack. The Kwantung Army in Manchuria was emptied out, being dispatched to places like the Philippines and Okinawa. Japanese living in Manchuria were drafted to fill in the ranks, so there was no real Kwantung Army force in Manchuria at the time. Most were not well-educated. Ishii's idea was that when the Russians attacked, we would drop bacteriological weapons from the air and spread disease. His plan was to accumulate three hundred thousand rats, and fleas.

The American navy was attacked at Pearl Harbor, and the Japanese thought it was a victorious strike. Yet, within two years, America had built up its naval strength again. America is a machine society. But bacteriological warfare does not rely on machinery. So Ishii's idea was to kill all the attacking Russians with disease. Once killed, troops are not rebuilt like machinery. The Japanese army promised Chinese children money for bringing in rats, but later gave them a pencil for every rat. The end purpose of all this effort was war. In war, the side who kills more people wins. Bacteria can kill on a large scale, so Ishii pressed this forward.

Former *kenpeitai* buddies and I used to meet to drink,

and we would talk about the war days. But nobody ever spoke about sending people to Unit 731. And of course the children were never told. I knew that what we did was wrong and did not want to tell my family about it. Then, one day, I called my family together—children and grandchildren—and told them that I was going to testify about what I did during the war. The was the first time I said anything about it. Overcoming my reluctance to speak that first time made it possible for me to tell my story repeatedly.

I was reading the impressions written down by visitors to one of these Unit 731 exhibits. A thirteen-year-old girl wrote, "I apologize for the people killed by the Japanese."

And a nineteen-year-old boy wrote, "The government spends all its time talking about low-level matters. If we keep going this way, the same situation will happen again."

People criticize the youth of today for spending their time reading comic books and watching TV; grownups accuse them of not knowing what's going on in the world. But, they are aware. They know what's going on. And the grownups had better be aware, also.

We *kenpeitai* men sent three thousand people to their deaths in Unit 731. I pray for the repose of their souls.

———————————— ✳ ————————————

Army doctor (Yuasa Ken)

[This is a "composite" speech edited from several different talks given by the speaker. Yuasa spoke at several exhibitions around Japan in 1993 and 1994.]

This is not easy for me to speak about, but it is something I must confess. What I did was wrong. It is also true that it was forced on me by the government, but that does not reduce the size of my crime. It is something that happened a long time ago, but those who are not taught about the war are ill-educated.

A short while ago, the leader of the Social Democratic Party of Japan stated that Japanese aggression in China created twenty million [dead] victims. He later retracted that statement. There was no need for the retraction. The statement was true.

The Japanese army went to plunder and steal materials and to kill. Japan wanted iron, coal, and provisions, and the army drove into the mountains to prosecute the war. At the time, the Japanese used derogatory terms for the Chinese, like "Chinaman" and "Chink," and looked at them with contempt. When I was a child, we were told to despise the Chinese, despise the Koreans. "It's all right to conquer them. We have become elite, and should join with the Americans and British and conquer Asia." I hated war and killing, but around middle school and into college, I began to think that such ideas were unavoidable.

I was born into a doctor's family with a practice in our area. With the good fortune of that background, I graduated medical school. I wanted to serve in some village that had no doctor, or work in medical research, but circumstances did not permit it.

In 1941, I became a doctor and specialized in infectious diseases. I believed that under the emperor we were the greatest country in Asia. I became an army officer, different from ordinary people. I was proud to be under direct control of the emperor, and I was taught that if I believed in the emperor, my own happiness would come as an extension of that.

Some 1,700 or 1,800 of us from the Thirty-sixth Regiment in Iwate received training in hygiene, and in February 1942, we were sent overseas. Reflecting on it now brings the crime back to mind.

I was assigned to the army hospital in the southern part of Shanxi Province in China.

Why here? What was the purpose in carrying the war this deep into the country?

The purpose was robbery. Robbery was committed through use of equipment with high killing power. Kill anyone who resists, and use force to seize supplies, coal, and iron. And increase military power.

Shanxi Province had a population of thirty million. It was held by only sixty to seventy thousand Japanese troops through control of the cities, lines of communications, and railways. And in that way Japan stole its resources. It was an aggressive invasion, but we were forcibly indoctrinated to believe. That was the emperor system. The national anthem and the flag were awesome.

There was a railway line between our region and Dalian that was destroyed often by the Chinese. Japanese soldiers were stationed at places along the way, but there were vast stretches that could not be watched simulatneously. The People's Liberation Army used to come in and overturn trains and tear the rails apart. To prevent recurrences of such incidents, the Japanese army burned down the villages nearest to the damage. Or the villagers would be questioned about the whereabouts of the People's Liberation Army. Anyone who refused to answer was killed. This is how the entire country was occupied and held.

The Manchurian Incident of 1931 and the Marco

Polo Bridge Incident of 1937 happened under the pretext that we were protecting China from invasion by the U.S. and Great Britain. People were driven into a life in which human qualities were lost. The soldier's outlet for frustrations was the brothels of the comfort women. Any means was resorted to in order to raise one's rank and keep up the authority of the country. And in the army hospital, we practiced vivisection.

The battle line was being extended. We had to consider how to handle men who were wounded at the front. About half the army doctors did not know how to use a scalpel. Each method of treating sick and wounded soldiers at the front had a bearing on military strength. If men were sent behind the lines for treatment, it reduced the army's fighting strength considerably. One function of the army hospital was training doctors. Vivisection was used to practice for performing operations at the front lines. I operated on living Chinese for whom I had no hatred whatsoever to gain surgical ability in order to win the war.

The hospital I was assigned to was set up in an elementary school and a high school. There were seventy to eighty hygiene specialists, ten nurses, and ten army doctors and officers in our unit. Our job was to treat sick and wounded soldiers and send them back to the front lines.

One day I went into the school grounds. There were some Chinese soldiers of the resistance army and some peasants being held there, and Japanese soldiers were smoking and joking around among themselves. I still had a conscience then, and I asked if someone had done something bad enough to warrant an execution. The Japanese soldiers snickered derisively. "All resistance soldiers get executed," they answered. Living persons are good for scalpel practice, so people were brought in to the hospital by the *kenpeitai* to get cut up just like the *maruta* in Unit 731.

One day soon after I started at that assignment, the hospital head told us, "Today we will have surgery practice." I was startled. It was an order. There was no getting out of it. Normally, we dissected people who had died of such diseases as typhoid fever, dysentery, and tuberculosis. Now we were being taken to the dissection room for a different type of exercise. Soldiers came along as observers.

When we opened the door, there was a colonel waiting. We saluted. In the room were two Chinese who had been brought in by the *kenpeitai*. One looked like a soldier, the other was a farmer. There were two operating tables, and doctors and nurses; there were saws for cutting bones, and scissors and other equipment.

What did these people do? It must have been an act of patriotism. But I couldn't think about things like that back then. I only wanted to look good. We had an education in militarism, and in racism. We thought, "Ah! They surrendered to the Japanese army."

Everything started with a signal from the hospital head. One Chinese had big thighs and walked slowly and calmly. He lay down and had no sign of fear, no stress on his face. He was composed. Someone else used him for surgery practice.

I went over and pushed the other one to the operating table. I had no feeling of apology or of doing anything bad. The farmer was resigned to his fate, and he lowered his head and walked forward. I didn't want to get my clothes dirty from him; I wanted to look sharp. He went as far as the operating table but didn't want to lie down. A nurse using broken Chinese told him, "We're using ether; it won't hurt, so lie down." She gave me a wry smile when she said that. She had been working there for a long time, and when I happened to meet her again much later and asked her about it, she didn't remember. She was handling so many vivisections it was routine. People who repeat evil acts do not remember them. There is no sense of doing wrong.

War means this, also. War is not just shooting. In order for Japan to win, all the Chinese were made prisoners, women's bellies were cut open, homes were burned. If you couldn't do this, then you weren't a loyal soldier of the emperor.

The scene in the room was not a typical one of preparing for an operation, but a clamor. It was practice for army doctors for winning a war. If you made a disagreeable face, when you returned home you would be called a traitor or turncoat. If it were just me alone, I could tolerate it; but the insulting looks would be cast on parents and siblings. Even if one despises an act, one must bear it. From there, a person becomes accustomed to it.

We all received practice. It was normal to smile at this. The crimes committed during our aggressive wars are forgotten, gone from memory. At the time they were "right." If you are praised, you must go ahead and perform.

Surgery began. The man was given ether and dissected. His appendix was so small that it was like looking for a burrowing worm. I had to cut and search repeatedly. The blood flow was stopped, nerves were cut, bones were cut with a saw, and a tracheotomy was performed. Blood and air escaped from his body, and blood came foaming up. Practice time was two hours. The man died, and his body was thrown into a hole and buried. The burial area near the operating room was full, so we had to dig a hole farther away. We had received a request from a Japanese pharmaceutical manufacturer; I scraped samples from the outer covering of his brain, placed them into ten 500-cc bottles with alcohol, and sent them to the company for rheumatism research.

The other man, the soldier, was still panting. The hospital head used him for hypodermic practice and injected air into him. Then, to kill him, he injected the same liquid used for anesthesia.

That was my first crime. After that, it was easy. Eventually I dissected fourteen Chinese.

Once, I instructed a hygiene specialist in anatomy. We had charts and models, but I thought that actual experience would be faster. I contacted the *kenpeitai* and received one person. I cut the belly and the chest. I explained the intestines, the kidneys, the liver, and the stomach—I was doing hideous things.

I also saw vivisections. Once I saw about forty doctors gathered. There was a man bound and squatting. The guard asked the doctors, "Are you ready?" and the prisoner was laid out and, without anesthetic, two cuts were made down his belly. The victim made a few gasps—the dissection was a botch—and he died soon. I saw four people dissected that way.

Once, at the Shanxi First Army Headquarters, there were some forty army doctors gathered from base and field hospitals. There was a lecture on military medicine, and afterward we were led to the prison cells. There were two Chinese in a cell. The jailer took out his pistol and fired two shots into each of their bellies. One of them was vivisected right there in the room. There was no anesthesia. While this was going on I heard four more shots fired. That meant two more people. Our object was to keep the person alive until the bullets were removed. Since we neither tried to administer ether nor stop the flow of blood, the men died soon.

At Unit 731, the special team carried out tests with poisons at the ends of prison blocks 1 and 2. There was an iron door, and even unit members needed permission to enter here. The special team members startled me when I first saw their unusual manner of dress. They wore white coverall suits, army hats, rubber boots, and pistols strapped to their sides. They first came here to supervise the preliminary construction work of the facilities, then later became the Special Team. They even had their own quarters. They were all from around Ishii's hometown, and the leader was Ishii Shiro's elder brother.

A secret order came to the hospitals in northern China: "The war is not going well. Perform vivisections!" Thousands, or tens of thousands, of doctors used live subjects for dissection practice and research. What are those people doing now? Among the sixty or seventy thousand Japanese who went to China, forty to fifty thousand are still alive in Japan. There may be some feeling of shame, but most have forgotten. Soldiers went to the comfort women, and they raped them. Then, the next day, they would regain their strength to attack the Chinese. That's all forgotten in the Japan of today. I also believed that when I went to the comfort women I was merely paying for services. That was the level of my consciousness.

It is said that there were twenty million victims of the war in China. But only ten to twenty percent of these were killed in gunfire exchange. Most—non–resisting old people, women, and children—were captured and slaughtered. Prisoners of war could not be taken to the front or allowed to escape, so they were killed in the manner of the Rape of Nanjing.

Those who were part of it do not come forward to tell the people how it was. Why? Because the Japanese have all forgotten about it.

When I was captured in China, I did not realize my own crimes. I thought I had been taken prisoner only because Japan lost the war; the Japanese army's education was thorough. While I was confessing, I read what other people had written, and I realized that what they had done was wrong. But I also had been performing dissections on living people. Those who commit evil acts first wonder if anybody knows about it. The Chinese told me, "You came here because you were ordered to do so. But you yourself murdered. So write down everything honestly."

Prisoners who had committed light crimes were given two and a half years. More serious offenders were forwarded to another location, and their cases reviewed after three and a half years.

I spent eleven years in prison. Shortly before I was released, I received a letter from the aged mother of someone who was killed. She wrote, "I saw you people take him away. I was choked with emotion, and I ran after you with my bound feet. Later I learned that he was taken to the army hospital and cut up alive. I cried. I couldn't eat."

In July 1956, I was released from prison The person who came to meet me asked, "Why were you considered a war criminal? You were tough and you worked hard." I told him he was wrong, and reminded him that he did the same things in China, also. He said, "Oh, that," and he thought back and grimaced. That man died six years ago.

If I had not said anything about our past deeds, he would have died without realizing what he had done.

I was interviewed by a newspaper reporter at my home, and he commented that in spite of what I had done, I am still active as a doctor. "In Germany," he told me, "you would have been placed on trial."

It is not just the political and social sectors in Japan that ignore this past. The same tendency exists even in popular literature. European and American films take up the topic of soldiers who were in the Vietnam War coming down with psychological problems, developing neuroses, and even committing suicide. But in Japan, people who were guilty of atrocities in the war do not shudder from their crimes or commit suicide. It does not even happen in the popular literature. Why is it that, in this country, an offense is not considered a crime and people go on living without giving a second thought to such things? And in the midst of this, the economy has kept growing. This is Japan.

Twelve years ago I published a collection of my experiences in a book called *Unerasable Memories*. I gave copies to all my former army associates. Some people objected to my doing this, but at a gathering of former soldiers a while ago, an ex-high ranking officer commended me for it. "We did horrible things then," he said. "I can't say anything to my family, but I want to speak about it here. Let's get together every year."

Everybody forgot. They did "great" things and got medals, and they don't think they did anything worse than kicking a dog. I asked if anyone had nightmares about what he did, and nobody seemed bothered. People said that they had nightmares only when they were children and didn't have their homework ready for school.

They weren't bothered because they never considered it a dreadful thing to take a scalpel and cut open a living person.

The greatest crime, though, was not vivisection but joining the army as a medical doctor, treating sick and wounded soldiers to release them to fight again. This is the most criminal act: returning killer soldiers. The build-up of a big, invading army has been forgotten.

The present situation in Japan is cause for concern. Some people see a similarity with the 1930s. Are we now in a postwar era, or a prewar era? This is a strange atmosphere, and we are in the midst of a strange education.

❋

Civilian employee of Unit 731 in Tokyo (Ishibashi Naokata)

[Ishibashi, born in 1920, spoke both in person at Unit 731 exhibits and on videotape.]

I was a civilian assistant at the Japanese army's laboratory facilities in Tokyo, near where the bones were found in Shinjuku in 1989. It was the beginning of the second year after the China Incident of the summer of 1937, and since the war was being expanded I expected to go to the front in China, but only ten days after assuming my post in Tokyo, I was ordered to the Ishii unit in Harbin. There were seventeen or eighteen of us civilian employees in the army, both minors and adults. We left Tokyo in early November 1938.

I was assigned to a team under the leadership of an army doctor. Our job was to examine the *maruta* deliv-

ered to Unit 731 by the *kenpeitai*. We took samples of
their blood and stool, tested for kidney function, and
collected other physical data. This information was used
to determine a person's condition before the experiments. Without it, the data from bacteriological tests
could not be compared.

The *maruta* were supplied with good nutrition. They
were fed so as to give them the same physical endurance
as a soldier. Our team did not actually perform the tests
of infection through injection or through germ bombs.
Our work was similar to that of hospital technicians, so
after the war, some of my associates found work as
clinical technicians or X-ray technicians.

In 1940, from August through November, we were
planning for the plague attack on Ningbo. For our base,
we used an airfield at a former Chinese Nationalist Party
aviation school in Hangzhou at the mouth of the Tsien-
tang River. From there, light planes took the plague-
carrying fleas to Ningbo. They were slow planes, with
speeds of no more than one hundred eighty to two
hundred kilometers per hour, and I don't think they
could fly above four thousand meters. An attacking fight-
er could have brought them down in one shot, if there
had been an encounter. But no enemy planes came
around.

I know for sure there were fleas used in the drop.
Fleas were bred at Harbin and often flown into Hangzhou by a transport plane, and then they were transferred
to a light plane. Once, during a transfer, the fleas got
loose and got all over the airport. There was a scare that
everyone working in there would become infected, and a
lot of commotion followed. We sprayed large quantities
of insecticides over the airfield, and because of it extensive areas of grass died and turned a bright red.

Finally, the fleas were dumped on the port city of Ningbo. I heard that sorghum, wheat, and rice polishings were mixed with the fleas. We were at that former aviation school base for four months. I believe that was the first of the big scale biological warfare attacks.

During the time that the Ningbo attack was being planned, a group of us left Harbin by train for Hangzhou. It was a ten-day trip on a specially scheduled run. There were forty of us, and about the same number of men were coming by sea from Dalian by way of Shanghai. There were army doctors and hygiene specialist noncoms. From the Ei-1644 unit, the so-called Tama Unit in Nanjing, came a major general and several hygiene specialists. This was a joint operation.

The year before, in 1939, the Kwantung Army and the Soviets had clashed at Nomonhan. Japan used bacteria, and two of my friends who are still living now were involved in that operation. According to them, typhoid was thrown into a tributary of the Hailar River. I had stayed back at Pingfang, and a lot of unit members, from headquarters staff to noncoms, went to Nomonhan. The work load on those of us who stayed behind increased, and we had to cover jobs outside our regular work. At that time, I worked at cultivating typhoid bacteria.

As Professor Tsuneishi pointed out in his book, when these pathogens are thrown into a river, their ability to infect is quickly lost, so I never heard that we infected the Russian army. Ishii's Japanese-style thinking was wrong by a longshot. Wherever we Japanese go, we eat raw food and drink untreated water. But, the Chinese and the Russians do not drink water without boiling it.

During the time I was stationed at Hangzhou, prisoners were brought in by the *kenpeitai* and secret police and accused of being guerrillas or soldiers posing as civilians. One day, when it was almost suppertime, we heard there was going to be a dissection. I went outside to where it was scheduled. There was a hole dug in the ground, and two Chinese men were blindfolded and sitting on the ground by the hole. Then, two Japanese soldiers decapitated them. Blood from the carotid artery shot up two meters into the air, as if it were gushing from a hose. The heads rolled into the hole, and the bodies were dissected right there on the spot. As soon as they were killed, the chest cavity was opened and the heart was removed and placed on a scale for weighing. The heart was still beating, and it made the scale weights clank together.

The question is often asked why doctors who were supposed to be dedicated to saving people's lives ended up doing such evil deeds. I think it has to be seen against the background of the times. In 1937, when the Sino-Japanese War started, there was a pronouncement to the effect that the first reserve troops stationed in Manchuria would not be mobilized. The only exception would be if there were a major incident at the Soviet border with no time for sending in troops and equipment from the Japanese mainland. Civilian employees would not be called up, and the salary was better than back in Japan. Employees could bring their families to live with them, and people working in university medical labs in Japan could dispense with the worry of being drafted into military medicine. Even going to work in an army hospital would be relatively all right, but a doctor assigned to a combat unit could be sent out to battle zones where the bullets are flying.

I did not want to experiment on *maruta*. The major reason a lot of people joined was to protect health with hygiene, and the pay was good. At eighteen and nineteen years of age, we were getting higher salaries than the teachers who had educated us a long time ago, back in school.

Manchuria from 1938 to 1940 was like heaven for Japanese. We heard that on the mainland even matches were government-rationed, while we had plenty of everything. I was not so enthusiastic about becoming employed by the army, but the salary was a big attraction. When I worked on the Ningbo biological attack, I was getting a salary of one hundred twenty yen a month. In 1940, the principal of an elementary school did not make that much. The cost of living was low, and I would have been inducted into the military in another one or two years anyway. I saw a chance to rearrange my life starting from scratch.

I was in Unit 731 for two years and three months, up to the end of January 1940. After that, I was assigned to a border garrison.

Someone asked whether I had seen any woman *maruta*. Personally, I saw only two, in the Number 8 prison block. One was a twenty-one-year-old, married Chinese woman; the other was an unmarried Soviet girl of nineteen. I asked where she came from and learned that she was from the Ukraine, very far away. Those women were not used in any experiments during the time that I was there. They said that they had not seen their faces in a mirror since being captured, and they begged me to get them one. I sneaked a mirror to them and told them to be careful that the *kenpeitai* or the jail guards didn't see it.

✳

Youth Corps member attached to Unit 731
(Ogasawara Akira)

I joined the Youth Corps in 1943, on April 15. I was excited about airplanes, and I heard that if we went to the Kwantung Army headquarters we'd get to go up in a plane. I did not join Unit 731 from hearing about it and deciding to join. In May 1938, the year after the Sino-Japanese War started, my eldest brother was killed in action in Xuzhou. My school teacher told me "Go get your brother's enemy. You've got to go kill the Chinks!"

I took the exam for the Youth Air Corps School and passed. One week later I was contacted and told to report to the *kenpeitai* office in Shimonoseki. They called us together and the officer in charge said "All those who want to ride in a plane in the Kwantung Army, raise your hands." Some of us did, and then we were told to contact our families and advise them that we'd be leaving.

I thought the Kwantung Army meant the Tokyo area. [In Japan, a term using the same characters refers to the Tokyo-Yokohama area; Japanese used a term with those characters to refer to the eastern region of China.] Two or three hours later, we left the port of Shimonoseki. The next morning we were docking in Pusan, though I had no idea where we were. I looked out and thought it strange that there were so many people wearing Korean-style clothes. From the ship, we were taken to a train, and we started out toward Manchuria.

After we passed through Seoul, a lot of women boarded. Some of the fellows started teasing and making jokes about them, and they shot back, "We're going to work for the same Japanese army as you and you're making fun of us?" The sergeant in charge of our group told us that they were going to Manchuria to become comfort women, and we shouldn't fight with them.

We got to Changchun, and that's when I learned that that's where the headquarters of the Kwantung Army was located. We were interviewed, and four of us who were from the same area were ordered to Harbin.

When I got there, I had another surprise. On the station platform there was a statue of Ito Hirobumi, the former Japanese resident general of Korea who was killed by the Korean An Chang Gun. People paid respects to the statue. That surprise has stayed with me until today.

[Ito was one of the founders of the new Japanese government after the Meiji Restoration of 1868. In the aftermath of her victory in the 1904–05 war with Russia, Japan occupied the Korean peninsula, and Ito took up the post of resident general in 1906. He thus became a symbol of oppression and was assassinated at Harbin Station in 1909. An Chang Gun was executed by the Japanese, and he became a hero to the Korean people. There is a memorial hall dedicated to him on the outskirts of Seoul.]

At one time I had the job of cleaning the human specimen room. There were medical charts of the *maruta* used in the plague attacks at Anda, and I started reading through them. Some would die in two days, some in five or seven, sometimes in ten days or more. It was clearly written that these were charts of people used in experiments that exposed them to attacks by plague-carrying fleas. The records showed that every month between forty and sixty people were killed in these plague tests. I was working diligently at raising those fleas, as I had been instructed to do. Because of my education in emperorism and militarism, I never thought that what I was doing was wrong.

Ten years ago, I moved to Hiroshima. I went to Peace Park and saw the message engraved there: "Sleep in peace. This mistake will never be repeated." I came to think that the mistake never to be repeated is not just the atomic bomb. The cruel and extremely inhuman behavior of Unit 731 must also never be repeated.

※

Professor emeritus at Osaka University (Nakagawa Yonezo)

[Nakagawa entered the medical department of Ishii Shiro's alma mater Kyoto Imperial University in 1945, going on, in later years, to become professor emeritus at Osaka University. The Japanese school year starts in April, so he had only a few months of student life before the war ended in August. This testimony is taken mainly from his address at the Unit 731 Exhibition in Osaka in the spring of 1994, supplemented by information he provided in personal meetings with the author.]

When we first started studying at Kyoto, our instructor was an army doctor who told us that the practice of medicine is not for healing the sick and injured. Japan, he said, was fighting the world, and medicine itself must become a weapon.

The instructor told us that animal tests alone were not sufficient for medical studies, and that human tests were also necessary. He said that such tests had actually been carried out, and showed us 16-mm movies that had been taken in Manchuria. One movie showed an experiment in which air was injected into the arms of living subjects to produce air embolisms. The films showed the victims in progressive stages of the condition, as they suffered to death.

Another film the instructor showed us was a beheading, with blood spurting from the body.

I believe that the Unit 731 research facilities were possibly the best in the world at the time. After they were blown up at the end of the war, the facts were revealed. This is a scar on Japanese medicine, but it goes beyond being a mere scar. Unit 731 came about as a result of the medical thinking in Japan.

Some of the experiments had nothing to do with advancing the capability of germ warfare, or of medicine. There is such a thing as professional curiosity: "What would happen if we did such and such?" What medical purpose would be served by performing and studying beheadings? None at all. That was just playing around. Professional people, too, like to play.

❋

Member of the Hygiene Corps (Tomioka Heihachiro)

[Tomioka served as a member on the Central Planning Committee for the Unit 731 Exhibition.]

In April 1940, I took the exam for the Hygiene Corps, and in December of that year I reported to my unit. We boarded a ship for China, where we began a four-month training period.

The object of training was to teach young people to be soldiers in the shortest possible time, and in order to do so, the men in charge hit the new recruits. There was not one day when we were not hit. Open-handed slapping does not hurt much, so they used fists. Sometimes, they would use the soles of *tabi* [Japanese-style footwear] so that the rubber treads would leave their marks on our faces. At times, they would use a belt, which was a little better; but sometimes they would use the buckle, and it would leave welts from the ear to the neck. Other times, they would use army boots, which have rivets on the soles. That would really knock you down.

So, we went from one day to the next getting hit as part of our training. Why did we get hit? Perhaps our clothes were dirty. Perhaps our shoes had not been properly taken care of. Perhaps we had dust on our rifles. We got hit every day. We had to wash the officers' underwear, and if we didn't do it right we'd get hit. If one person did something wrong, it was considered everybody's responsibility, so they would make us pair off facing each other, and we'd have to slap each other's faces. If we didn't slap hard enough, we'd get hit.

In a different kind of punishment, we'd have to hold ourselves up between two desks—one hand on each desk with our feet off the ground—then pedal as if in a bicycle race. Or, if we slipped up on something, they would make us display our shame to everybody by walking around to the different teams with a shoe in our mouths.

There was one type of rifle called a Type 38. It had the emperor's chrysanthemum crest on the front end. We were taught that each rifle was lent to us by the emperor, and that we had to treat it with respect. If we handled it wrong, or in a manner that was not befitting its status, we were made to stand with the rifle at present arms, holding it with arms stretched out front, at shoulder height. We would have to stay that way for one or two hours, until given the order to put our arms down. That was rough; the rifle weighed about three kilograms.

Every day, without fail, we would get hit. And that's where the spirit of absolute obedience is born. It's like training a dog. Humans and animals are the same. If you hit them, they learn to obey.

One day we were told that instead of using straw dummies for bayonet practice we would use people. We were going to practice on five people who had been brought in by the *kenpeitai*. We were told that they were members of the anti-Japanese resistance movement, but when they brought in the prisoners, they were seventeen or eighteen years old.

We were lined up in columns according to our unit, and the prisoners were tied in place. We were ordered to fix our bayonets. The boy at the front of the line was first. The commanding officer gave the orders: Forward! Back! Forward! Thrust!

This was the first time I'd killed anyone. My legs were shaking. When you thrust, it should be done fast. I was afraid, though, and I closed my eyes, so I don't know where I stuck the person. About twenty-five of us in turn, one after the other, stuck the prisoner. By that time, his shirt looked like a beehive with flat holes instead of round ones. That's how we killed. There was a concept in our education that one does not become an adult until he has killed someone.

Before that boy's breathing stopped, I heard him crying, "Mama, mama," and I realized that it's the same in China as in Japan.

That is how we killed five Chinese for bayonet practice. After it was over, we threw the bodies into a pit and buried them. The location was at a mountain with no farms or anything else around. I never went back there again, and I have no idea what happened to the bodies after that.

And that was the education for the Youth Corps. One does not become an adult without killing.

About four months after that, we were transferred to another camp. The commander there asked us if we had ever killed anyone. We told him that yes, we had done it in our training course. He scoffed, saying that killing only one person didn't mean much. He said that there were two prisoners there right then, and told us we had to kill them. It was unavoidable, so we started by digging a hole. A prisoner of about forty years old who looked like a farmer was brought out. The officer commanded me, "Kill him!"

The prisoner was not tied to a post, but was just standing with his hands tied behind his back. When I thrusted, the bayonet did not enter his body, and he fell to the ground. The unit officer screamed at me, "Do you think you can kill a man like that?" And to show me how to do it, he demonstrated by killing the man with a single thrust. One could see that the unit leader was good. I followed his example and killed the other farmer, then dragged his body to the hole and buried him.

Then, I had night watch in a high guard tower. The place where we killed the Chinese was right in front of the tower, and I was afraid to look in that direction. Most of the time I looked the other way. There was even a time during which I felt haunted, afraid that a ghost might come out from there.

This is the way my training went, with my killing one or two people at a time until over five years I had finally, as an individual, killed a total of thirty-three people directly. In unison with others, I was party to the killings of more than seven hundred people. Sometimes a locality would be surrounded and then attacked, and it is not possible to know which person was killed by which soldier, but I share the responsibility, and I want to testify here to these facts also.

In 1942, our unit took part in a siege in Shantung Province. We encircled an area with a circumference of one hundred sixty kilometers and conducted what we called a "rabbit hunt" inside the encircled area. At night, troops climbed mountains and traversed rivers with flaming torches. Everywhere one looked, the torches were burning. Our intention was that not one "rabbit" should escape. All the men we captured in that operation— young and old, alike—were made to march to the train. From there, they were put into freight cars and taken to Japan, where they were sacrificed working in the Hanaoka mines.

[Koreans and Chinese were brought in and beaten into forced labor at the Hanaoka mines to produce fuel for Japan's war machine. As in other Japanese forced-labor projects, such as the Burma-Siam Railroad, the death rate was high. Books and articles on the Hanaoka mines have appeared over the years, but redress from the government seems as remote as it has been with the comfort women problem.]

There were other mines in different parts of Japan, also, where such people were forced to work on meager rations. Many of them died from malnutrition. The people that we captured and sent off to be laborers were among them.

That was not the only destination for the prisoners we took. Other people giving testimony at this exhibition have spoken of the *maruta,* and one person who testified here earlier mentioned that an unusually high percentage of the Chinese *maruta* came from Shantung Province. That large number from Shantung Province is because of the prisoners that we took and sent to Unit 731 for their experimentation.

Another time, we took eight prisoners who had raised a white flag and surrendered. We were told to take them to a farm and wait there. I was wondering how we were going to transport them, when night came and we received orders to kill them. They were sitting on the ground, and the young soldiers like myself were ordered to bayonet them from the front while the experienced soldiers held the prisoners' shoulders from behind. After we killed them, we just left them there on the ground and went back to the battlefront. We didn't even dig holes.

This was one example of the conduct of the Japanese army, and it was absolutely against international law.

※

Soldier stationed at Pingfang (Shinohara Tsuruo)

Unit 731 was an underground organization. We were told to take the secret to the grave with us, and many people did adhere to the order for years after the war. But now, thanks to these times of peace, those who believed in the homeland and sacrificed themselves for it should not be forgotten. Truth is often recorded by being handed down verbally, and I believe that we cannot leave a blank space in history. For that reason, I summon up the courage to stand before you now to tell the truth about what I saw at Unit 731.

In December 1944, I was nineteen years old and

working in Manchuria for the South Manchuria Railway Company, when an order for mobilization came from the Kwantung Army. Early the following year, I received orders to go to Harbin. I was told to go to the station at Harbin at a specified date and time and wait by the statue of Ito Hirobumi.

The train pulled in, and there were others already waiting there. A soldier came to take charge of us, and we boarded a train and went one stop to a small station. We got out at a tiny, remote village. That was Pingfang. On the horizon, there was a huge edifice that looked like one could put Tokyo's Marunouchi Building inside it three times.

We got off the train. In front of the station there were two soldiers working with something that looked like a fireman's hose, drawing up water from the river into buckets. Our leader told us, "This is river water, and there's no bacteria in it. Do you fellows want to take a drink?" We passed it up and kept walking. In hindsight, it must have been the Ishii water purifier they were working with, making the water safe for drinking.

We walked up the hill to the front of the unit and fell into formation in front of the main gate. Major General Kikuike, the adjutant, addressed us. The first thing he said was, "You fellows! Look behind me! Do you notice anything?"

We all said no, and he continued.

"There is no imperial chrysanthemum crest on the front of this unit." None of us had thought of that. All other installations displayed the crest at their entrances, and Japanese naval ships had the crest displayed at their bows. The adjutant continued speaking, advising us that "in due time, as the days pass, you'll get to learn what this unit is all about."

We were issued our uniforms and instructions. Then, as Unit 731 members, we received textbooks and were given an education that was made to penetrate into our bodies. We were told that our classes would start the next day, and that those of us who showed exceptional spirit would be recommended for assignment to the medical hospital in Harbin.

We all set to work with the ambition of studying diligently and making the best of our situation. We went on a hard schedule: from eight in the morning until midnight, with the exception of lunch and supper, we were in class. We were drilled in a scientific curriculum that included courses in human anatomy, disease prevention in the military, army hygiene, the Ishii system of water purification, the essentials of river water supply, emergency disinfection including emergency antidotes for poisoning, disease prevention patrol, and water testing patrol. These are the subjects we had to absorb in a short time.

Our instructor told us about the situation with the war—that Japan was losing. The unit leader came around during instruction period and told us, "Education is like your own internal organs. It brings out your ability. So I want you to apply yourselves."

Studying under a schedule like this every day, it was only natural that in the afternoons we would get sleepy. The instructor woke us up by telling us stories about his own experiences. Once, he recalled the time when he was part of an operation in the city of Jilin. They carried plague bacteria there and conducted tests. The method involved placing the pathogens into buns and then wrapping them in paper. The Unit 731 men went to an area of the city where children were playing, and started eating buns similar to those in which they had planted the germs. The children saw the men eating, and came over. Then, the men gave the children the infected buns. Two or three days later, the strategy team went to the village to investigate, and noted stories about outbreaks of disease.

There were vegetable gardens at the unit. Gardens on one side were for growing food for us; the gardens on the other side were used for testing cholera germs for use as plant pathogens, but I heard later that those tests ended in failure.

People who were arrested on the Chinese mainland as spies, then tried in a military court in Harbin and found guilty, were sent to Unit 731 and placed into prison blocks for medical experiments There were always guards at the entrance. Every day, a covered truck came in from Harbin with three or four *maruta*. Our instructor told us that, in the prison blocks, the *maruta* were being infected with plague, cholera, typhus, and syphilis. He said that one test entailed injecting typhoid germs into a person's side. We did not have the authority to enter the blocks and could only hear about what went on inside from our instructor. He related that, on entering the dissection room, one first had to put on heavy rubber clothes, then a disinfectant mist was sprayed from above. He said that about three or four people at a time worked on a dissection. While one person worked with the scalpel, another next to him measured time—for example, how much time elapsed from injection until dehydration set in, and how long it would take for death to occur.

I thought that this was a cruel thing that the Japanese army was doing, but that I had to resign myself to it.

In July, we heard news that the Special Attack Forces [the kamikaze and other suicide units] would be taking off from the Unit 731 airfield. If we were called to go, we would have to resign ourselves to death. I would have been resigned to my fate, in line with the teachings of the Buddhist saint, Amida.

In August, a message came to the unit that Sato Take, the Japanese ambassador to Moscow, had gone to speak with Molotov with a request for peace. On the morning of the ninth, Molotov's reply came: at midnight, the Soviets would invade Manchuria. This message went to the War Ministry, which in turn ordered us to "stop 731 research. Blow up facilities immediately and evacuate."

Early the next morning, we started the job of evacuation. About one hundred people pulled out first and headed for the Korean border. Unit 731 got the Russian message before any other unit, but we did not know whether Molotov's statement was true or not, so the *maruta* were not killed yet.

At the morning muster on August 9, an officer on a white horse galloped around the compound telling us that the Soviets had attacked, and we were to pay close attention to unit orders from now on. The first thing we were told to do was destroy any evidence on us that we were connected with Unit 731. The next day, three of us were assigned to go into the prison blocks. This was an area I had been prohibited from entering until now. In one block, three *maruta* were lying on the floor, but most of them had already been taken outside. We dug a hole and piled up several alternating layers of logs and *maruta*, one on top of the other. None of us knew what the other people were doing; we each worked in our own group. The upper-ranking officers sent their families, along with their important documents, to Tokyo from the Unit 731 airfield. The unit leader's house was in Tokyo, and I think that that's where the documents were all taken.

We had to blow up the prison cells. They were numbered 1 through 12. I went into the Number 12 cell to place explosives into the walls. The walls were white, and on one there was a message written in blood: "Down with Japanese imperialism. Long live President Jiang [Chiang]!" The blood had not darkened yet, so it had to have been written very recently. And it was written in educated script. Whoever wrote that had obviously cut his finger to get the blood. He was undoubtedly suffering from experiments and on the verge of death. Those characters will remain with me for life; they are etched into my heart.

I thought that the person in that cell must have been a key figure directly under the authority of Jiang Jieshi. I ran outside, but the layers of firewood and *maruta* were already piled up. I looked for someone with blood on his hands that would indicate who he was, but I was not able to find him.

On August 14, at 6 P.M., the order came to blow up Unit 731. The laboratory equipment and the specimens in the glass cases were being loaded onto trucks from the evening of the thirteenth, and through the next morning, numerous trips were made to the Songhua [Sungari] River to dump the specimens. Most of the unit members pulled out, and there were only about thirty people left when the facilities were blown up. Before the facilities were blown up, I went through the different cells for a farewell look. There was not even one item to be seen in any cell. Everything had been stripped bare.

The switch to set off the charges was thrown, and we boarded the train with the sound of explosions ringing in the air.

We headed south, toward the northern border of Korea, picked up the advance group that had left the grounds ahead of us, and started crossing the Korean peninsula.

The fifteenth and sixteenth passed without incident. On the train, an officer came and told us "On September 1, you men will fly to Okinawa and spread bacteria among the American forces. You will be the *Yozakura* Special Forces." We were carrying bacteriological bombs with us on the train, but they ended up being disposed of in the Sea of Japan. After that, the local situation became restless, and guns were set up in the freight cars. We reached Pusan on the twentieth, and from there we were placed on a ship for Japan, eventually docking in Yamaguchi Prefecture. Then, we scattered like butterflies and returned to our hometowns.

Later, I found a job on the Japanese National Railways. On January 26, 1946, there was a detestable incident at a branch of the Teikoku Bank. A man faked the identity of an official from the Ministry of Health and Welfare and appeared at a branch of the bank. He told the manager that an epidemic disease had broken out in the vicinity and asked to have all the employees gather for instructions on how to drink a preventive medicine. Twelve people died, and the police went searching for the culprit.

It was natural that Unit 731 should fall under the eyes of investigators. Detectives came to my place of work and told me, "You were in Unit 731. Your superior officers gave you potassium cyanide to drink in case you were captured by the Russians or Americans." I was shocked. I said I didn't know anything about it and tried to brush it off. From then on, the detectives kept coming back and talking to my superiors. Talk spread around my workplace that I was a war criminal, and that I did not have the right to work in a public organization. I started getting dirty looks. I quit the national railways and wandered around for a while. Then, in September 1951, the peace treaty was signed in San Francisco, and the post-war period became more settled. I didn't think anybody would be bad-mouthing me any more, so I decided to go into business for myself and have continued that way ever since.

———————————————— ✳ ————————————————

Soldier attached to Unit 731 (Ohara Takeyoshi)

I joined the cavalry in my home prefecture in 1939. In April of that year, I was stationed in Northeast China, then in March 1942, I was transferred to Unit 731. I did not know anything about that unit. My orders were for transfer to the Epidemic Prevention and Water Supply Unit Headquarters. In time, I found out what Unit 731 really was.

My first duty was taking care of domesticated animals, such as sheep, goats, horses, and cows. I assisted in researching the diseases that affect these animals.

At Anda, I saw tests in which *maruta* were tied to crosses in a large circle, as planes flew over and dropped bacteriological bombs in the area surrounded by the crosses. Their legs were chained, and their bodies were tied tightly; we observed the tests from a distance of about two hundred meters.

I had the job of cleaning up and disinfecting after the experiments, and gathering debris lying around. We wore special clothes that had a zipper in front and covered us from head to toe. We wore gas masks, rubber boots, and rubber gloves. Since we'd go into bacteria infested areas, we couldn't go to the toilet because of the danger of our getting infected ourselves. We'd have to go back to the unit, get into a tent for a disinfectant shower over our rubber clothes, and then wait a while. After that, we could finally take off the protective clothing. Then, we'd have to get into a disinfectant bath, then another bath with different water. When that was over, we could at last get dressed. I didn't know what kind of bacteria was being used at the Anda testing ground.

I want people who come to this exhibition to tell their children and grandchildren that there is nothing more stupid and fearful than war.

--------------------------------- ✳ ---------------------------------

Nurse attached to Unit 731 (Sakumoto Shizui)

There was a hospital in Harbin for treating members of Unit 731 who became sick or infected from working with the experiments. I was assigned there in the summer of 1942, and I worked there for about a year. People infected with plague were also sent to us. With plague, as you know, many people die in three days to a week after infection occurs.

When I was there, a nineteen-year-old by the name of Ishii Ichiro [almost certainly General Ishii's son] who had contracted plague was sent to us from headquarters. Plague is a very serious problem, so all communicable disease cases in our hospital were taken to another hospital. There were twenty-five of us nurses, and five of us were picked to take care of Ishii. There's no telling when a patient like this could die. The medical officer in charge told us, "If he has a lung hemorrhage, you get outside quickly." But there was no coughing up of blood, and in a month the patient recovered.

During that month, we all worked with the feeling that we never knew who among us might be the next one to be sacrificed. We couldn't eat. And, when we had night duty, we had to stay in the same room with the patient. Thinking about it now, that was fearful work. But I came through it, and I've lived a long life.

When we were first called to serve, it was for a hospital ship. That was in July 1941. With the outbreak of the war, it was decided that hospital ship duty would be too dangerous for women, and they transferred us to land units. I worked in an army hospital for a year, and then received a transfer to Harbin. Nobody knew anything about communicable diseases there, or about a special unit. With no advance notice, we were transferred to the south wing of the hospital. I now know how highly secret it was.

---

*

Intelligence officer (Ogura Yoshikuma)

I joined the army in my home prefecture of Kagoshima, and later was sent to Tokyo. In preparation for the southward expansion of operations, I was assigned to study Islam; at the time there was confusion between Islam and Judaism. After that I was sent to Manchuria and assigned to a unit directly under the control of General Staff Headquarters, Special Forces. In other words, we were spies.

My first assignment was in Harbin, and after that I went to other areas. During that time my work involved gathering information from the Soviet Union and on biological warfare strategy.

Right after I reached Manchuria in 1939, the Nomonhan Incident occurred. That was when Japan first employed bacteriological warfare, dumping typhus germs into a river. The effect on the enemy was doubtful, but there were casualties among the Japanese army itself.

I was stationed in a location called Dongning. The leadership there had absolute authority in Manchuria. The place was situated between an old Soviet army base and a Kwantung Army base. The people of the village had been chased out, and only the church was left standing. The reason for leaving the church was that the Soviets who used it might come there.

Usually, we did not carry guns and lived like ordinary civilians, gathering information on the Soviets. In one year, I wore a uniform only once. Even going in and out of Unit 731, I was in civilian clothes.

In order to gather information, we used Manchurians with some degree of education and trained them for a short time, then sent them into the Soviet Union to do intelligence work. Those people, however, would be used by the Soviets for counterintelligence and sent back to Manchuria. And this is how intelligence was gathered, through this coming and going of Manchurian agents.

I think that the Soviets were far superior to us at gathering intelligence. They had non-rotating staff doing only intelligence work. The Manchurian spies they sent were so well trained they never gave themselves away. And the Soviets were better than us at code-breaking.

I was also involved with bacteriological tactics. I went in and out of Unit 731 repeatedly, and I saw experiments carried out on humans. I used to carry back bacteria from Unit 731, inject them into pigs and other domestic animals, and release the animals into Soviet territory. And it was not only animals. I used people also. We would inject people, wait two or three days, take them up to Soviet border, and send them in. When we went up near the border at night, the Soviets would shoot illuminating shells and then open up with gunfire. That was dangerous work.

There were also what we called "Q" operations. We would fill balloons with nitrogen and suspend containers of bacteria below them. They would be released to drift over Soviet territory to disperse bacteria. We never found out what effects this tactic had.

Why did the Japanese army research and develop bacteriological weapons? It was a way to kill a large number of people at low cost. The Geneva Convention's ban on biological warfare also caught the eyes of the Japanese. Unit 731's research did not produce many weapons for actual war, but mainly conducted research that was of no practical use, such as studying what happens when pathogens are injected directly into a person, and removing the organs of a healthy person for study.

These days, North Korea is receiving attention from the media. When I was serving in China, Kim Il Sung was fighting against Japan's setting up the puppet state in Northeast China. We chased Kim for more than a year and devised plans to capture him, but we never succeeded. When I hear his name it brings back memories.

For fifty years, I said nothing about my experiences; I heard about the Unit 731 Exhibition here and came to see it. That made me remember those times and finally gave me the impetus to speak about what happened back then.

When we lost the war, the Chinese who had been my subordinates were friendly toward me. They said that Japan had been burned and razed flat, and that I'd be better off staying there than returning home. But I headed home and they helped me clear out when I left.

The Manchurians must already have known about Japan's losing the war when I first heard about it. They already had documents for appointments issued by either the army of Jiang Jieshi or Mao Zedong. We Japanese knew nothing about what was happening. Looking back at it now, it seems like a joke.

———————————— ✳ ————————————

[In 1981, two reporters from the Mainichi *newspaper sought out former members of Unit 731 for interviews. They concluded their coverage by noting that "naturally, some people did not want to talk. Some former members we approached said, 'You're mistaking me for someone else.' At the homes of others, they said, 'I can't talk about that,' and sent us away. One former technician, a lieutenant during the war, said that he would talk with us, but not in the house, so we interviewed him standing outside."*

The interviews were carried in the November 27 issue of the newspaper. The following testimonies are excerpted from this article.]

Army major and pharmacist attached to Unit 731 (Anonymous)

[This resident of Hyogo Prefecture was sixty-six years old at the time of the interview. After the war, he went on to become the head of a medical research laboratory]

In April 1942, Units 731 and 516 joined together for tests near the Soviet border on the outskirts of the city of Hailar. The tests lasted three days and used approximately one hundred *maruta*. Four pillboxes were used, and two to three *maruta* were placed in a pillbox at a time for each test. Electrodes were placed on the victims and a desk and monitoring equipment were set up about fifty meters away.

Canisters of liquefied phosgene gas were thrown into the pillbox. As the gas spread and asphyxiated the victims, changes in their pulses and other vital signs were observed and recorded up until death occurred.

When death was confirmed, the officers went to the pillbox, checking for residual gas with litmus paper, and pulled out the bodies. A *maruta* who happened to survive was put through the test once again. There were no survivors. A tent was set up nearby where the dead were dissected.

One *maruta* was a sixty-eight-year-old man. Back at Unit 731, he had been injected with plague germs but did not die. He was put through the phosgene gas test and survived. An army doctor injected air into his veins, and he still did not die. The doctor then used an extra-heavy needle, and again injected air into the vein, but the man still survived. Finally, the doctors killed him by hanging him by the neck from a tree.

I remember the voices of surprise from the doctors when they dissected him. His internal organs were comparable to those of a young man.

One time, I saw a technician at Unit 731, a field-grade officer, carrying out tests aimed at combating frostbite. [The *Mainichi* article reported that the name of the technician was given, though it was not revealed in the article.] Five White Russian women were used in the test at the time.

The technician placed the women's hands into a freezing apparatus and lowered its temperature to minus ten degrees Celsius, then slowly reduced the temperature to minus seventy degrees. The condition of the frostbite was then studied.

The result of the test was that the flesh fell from the women's hands, and the bones were exposed. One of the women had given birth in prison, and the baby was also used in a frostbite test.

A little later, I went to look into the women's cells, and they were all empty. I assume that they died.

Army major and technician attached to Unit 516 (Anonymous)

[At the time of the interview, this man was a professor emeritus at a national university.]

In 1943, I attended a poison gas test conducted jointly by Units 731 and 516. It was held at the Unit 731 test facilities, east of Harbin. A glass-walled chamber about three meters square and two meters high was used. Inside of it, a Chinese man was blindfolded, with his hands tied around a post behind him. The gas was adamsite [sneezing gas], and as the gas filled the chamber the man went into violent coughing convulsions and began to suffer excruciating pain. More than ten doctors and technicians from the two units were present. After I had watched for about ten minutes, I could not stand it any more, and left the area. I understand that other types of gasses were also tested there.

Ishii Shiro's driver (Koshi Sadao)

[Koshi, who lost his own son to stray plague germs, has testified on video, on TV programs, and in person at the exhibitions. Part of his work included repeated trips to the gas chamber with a truck, each time carrying about ten maruta—and often with Ishii at his side. The gas chamber was a small installation inside a large building.]

There were different kinds of gas used for the tests. Mustard gas, lewisite, cyanic acid gas, and phosgene gas were all among the gases tested. Three of the chamber walls were glass, so that the conditions under which the victims died could be observed closely. Some of the *maruta* were tied to a dolly that rode on rails into the chamber. Then, the gas was piped in. We experimented with different concentrations. Photos and movies were taken, and very careful notes were made, such as what sort of symptoms a subject exhibited at how many seconds of inhalation. When the gas took effect, people would foam at the mouth.

A person's respiratory organs are similar to those of a pigeon. Generally, a person can maintain life in a given environment if a pigeon can. So pigeons were put into the chamber with the *maruta* as a comparison test. Sometimes, dogs were put in. All sorts of comparison tests were made.

At the Anda biological warfare bomb testing ground, we watched through binoculars from a distance of about four kilometers. There was very little sound when the bomb hit. Then, the contents released, appearing smoky. There was no gunpowder explosion that would kill the fleas. Each *maruta* had a head protector and a chest protector to prevent being killed by the bomb fragments. If bomb shrapnel were to get them, then the effects of the bacteria could not be evaluated. Only the arms and legs were exposed. Afterward, the progress of the plague through the body was observed.

Once, a *maruta* got loose, and, one after the other, they untied each other and began running away. Just about all forty of them scattered over the field. But there was no place to escape to by that remote airport. There was nothing else to do but get in the truck and run over them. Sometimes, I'd get one under the front; sometimes, I'd feel one crushed under the running board. In the end, all forty were killed.

Around June 1945, we knew that things were coming to an end. About that time, one day a truckload of about forty Russians came in. There were a lot of *maruta* already on hand, and there would be no need for them. So, the Russians were told that there was an epidemic in the region, and that they should get off the truck to get preventive injections. Then, they were injected with potassium cyanide. The men administering the injections rubbed the arms of the Russians with alcohol first. If you're going to kill someone, there's no need to disinfect the injection area; that was just to conceal the real intention. It only took a small amount, and even those big Russians fell back as soon as the injection was given. They didn't even make a sound—they just dropped.

✳

Pharmacist attached to the laboratory at Dalian (Meguro Masahiko)

The last time I saw Ishii was at Dalian, around August 10, 1945. Everybody was gone, except for four or five people who stayed behind to blow up the buildings. Ishii wanted pictures of the site taken after the buildings were destroyed. He said he needed them for the Army Ministry. Large quantities of photos were taken and developed before Ishii left. He took the photos and flew to Tokyo.

After the war, there were fantastic payments to former Unit 731 members. Some people got up to two million yen. That kind of money was unheard of in those days, around 1948 or 1949. It was unbelievable. Maybe the American army brought it in: I don't know where it came from, but, almost without exception, anyone connected in any way at all with Unit 731 got something. That was the best-paying job there was.

A lot of university professors were connected with Unit 731. Especially upper-level people, like in the Ministry of Health and Welfare and those concerned with vaccines. They all had some connection with the Ishii unit in some way. They never said anything about it, but they all received pay for working there. Those are the people who built the foundation of today's Japan.

✳

Captain, Japanese Imperial Army (Kojima Takeo)

[Kojima spoke at Tsukuba City in Ibaraki Prefecture.]

Perhaps there are some people here at this Unit 731 Exhibition who think that this was all there was to Japanese aggression at the time. Unit 731 was merely one segment of the dark shadow of Japan's aggression, and I would like to tell of my experience in this.

I graduated university in 1939, and in December of that year I joined the army. I was sent to the Kwantung Army in Shantung Province, where I spent six years, until the end of the war.

I learned Russian, and in May 1945, I was transferred to Intelligence, where I spent four months gathering data and listening in on and decoding Russian messages. After four months of this, it was as good as knowing nothing at all. Finally, they attacked. When they did, they did not use any coded telegraphic terms or coded text in their communications. Everything was sent in normal Russian.

We established the location of the Russian incursion with radio direction finders. We knew that after crossing the border, they had made a quick advance of eighty kilometers. That distance meant that they were not infantry, but mechanized units. Shortly after the attack, we retreated to the Korean border. There, I was captured and sent to a camp in Siberia. I was there for three years, and for two years after that I was transferred from one camp to another.

I was in the army for six years, and Siberia for five. In October 1949, the present country of China was born. Of the Japanese who had been in China and were then being held prisoner in Russia, 1,050 of us who were designated war criminals were sent back to China. We were incarcerated in a camp together with Chinese who were also considered war criminals, such as those who had served under Pu Yi or his brother. Among these approximately one hundred prisoners was the transportation minister of the puppet state of Manzhouguo.

I spent another six years in China. Finally, after seventeen years, I came back to Japan. I had joined the service at twenty-two years of age and returned home at thirtynine.

We were born and raised in a society of emperorism. A person's absolute responsibility above the army and government was to the emperor. The emperor was a living deity. The emperor's command was supreme and controlled the entire country. We were told how we must serve the emperor, how we should behave toward our parents, how we should behave toward our teachers, and how we should behave toward our siblings. We were taught that Japan is a sacred country, that the people of

Japan are a superior race, that the people of China, Korea, Southeast Asia, and Russia were all inferior races, and the superior race must govern them. And, by doing so, we would bring them happiness. This was the cause to which Japan must devote itself. In addition, shrines were built all over the country, and we all professed loyalty to the country and the emperor. This was our prewar education.

The purpose of the war, to put it bluntly, was to gain natural resources and create a market in the occupied lands for Japanese goods. The eight hundred thousand troops of the Kwantung Army in Manchuria were all self-sufficient from the land. With certain, limited exceptions, even arms were produced there. In order to form an army close to the border, seventy thousand Chinese were forced into service to help us hold our positions. This information could not be allowed to be released, so later these Chinese were all killed in mass executions and buried. In later years, with the building boom in Manchuria, bones have been unearthed at construction sites.

Soon after we went into the service, we were given training to get our courage up. We were ordered to watch beheadings. Chinese were made to sit by a hole in the ground, and the seasoned soldiers would cut their heads off. Blood spurted up from the neck into the air, and the bodies would roll into the holes.

Then we had bayonet practice. Victims had their hands tied behind them around a tree, and were used as bayonet targets. We had to watch this as part of training. This was a shock to me, and for two or three days, food would not pass through my throat. But, two years later, I became an officer in charge of a platoon, with about twenty-five men under me. Later, I became a company commander with one hundred fifty men, and that meant that if I didn't build strong platoons and a strong company, I would fall behind. And so I, too, tested the courage of the soldiers under me by using Chinese prisoners. This was normal training in the Japanese army.

In my first experience in battle, we were about to move into the combat zone. The Chinese knew we were coming, and their soldiers took off their uniforms and dressed like farmers. We couldn't tell farmers from soldiers, so our orders were to kill any men we came across.

We traveled through the night, and by dawn we were approaching the combat area. Also at dawn, farmers were leaving their homes and heading for the fields. My men killed them. Some were cut down with swords by soldiers on horseback. If we saw farmers working in the fields, we shot them.

What I will talk about next is something that is extremely difficult for me to say before you. Once, when I was leading my soldiers along the banks of the Yellow River, we came across a solitary house. My men opened the door, and there was an old man, a young couple, and two children inside. They looked at me with terror in their eyes. I ordered my men to kill them. The soldiers lined them up side by side—the old man, the married couple, a boy about ten years old, and another boy about seven—and shot them.

The next day, I thought I'd check the house. The old man, the couple, and the older child were dead. The seven-year-old boy was sprawled out face up on the earthen floor, staring at me. I just turned and left the house. Things like these were normal, daily occurrences. This was just one operation.

From 1942, the Japanese war front expanded, and there was a shortage of labor. It was difficult for Japan to meet production requirements. So it was decided to round up able-bodied Chinese and send them to Japan as laborers. We held meetings for about a month to figure out how this could be done. It was like moving pieces around on a game board.

The method we decided on was another field operation. We established a circle thirty-two kilometers in diameter encompassing entire villages and settlements. We then lined the circumference with several tens of thousands of soldiers. The troops started moving into the circle, pressing everyone in toward the center, just as if we were on a rabbit hunt. We had a tank corps in reserve in case a settlement put up strong resistance. When there was a village or settlement up ahead, I would fire off a machine gun, and that would scare everyone away from us and into the center. Whenever we could, we captured Chinese and handed them over to the *kenpeitai* officers. They would look the men over, pick out those who seemed able to do physical labor, tie their hands behind them, and then string them together like beads. We conducted this encircling operation three different times through the fields and mountains of the Shantung Peninsula, and rounded up some eight thousand Chinese. These records are in the archives of Japan's Self-Defense Agency in Tokyo.

In other operations, acting on orders from the commander of the army, we would pick out villagers at random—both old and young—and torture them to get information on where arms were hidden or being made. Then, we would kill them.

We also worked with Unit 731. Whenever we were out on an operation and an infectious disease broke out in a village, we would call off the operation, return to our base immediately, and receive inoculations. At times, we went into areas where cholera had broken out. We had

practiced for a week beforehand how to disinfect ourselves as quickly as possible after being exposed in such
areas. First, we would disinfect ourselves, then the weapons and the horses. We also disinfected our food. After
these training sessions, we worked in cholera-spreading
operations.

Cholera germs were introduced into the targeted area.
We would first determine that the disease had actually
broken out, and then move in. Whenever the Japanese
army moved in, the Chinese would always run away. As
they did, they spread the disease, and the cholera infected one person after the other and spread the disease,
according to our plan. The dead and those who couldn't
move were lying all around. It was summer, and they
were black with flies. It was a gruesome sight. We continued this operation for about two weeks, and the success
reports on the mission stated that about twenty thousand
Chinese died from cholera. There were 1,200 men in our
operation, and among these two hundred were identified
as carriers of the germ. Fifty of them developed cholera,
and five of them died. These five men, for some reason or
other, did not receive preventive inoculations. The ones
who were detected as carrying the germs were treated,
but it took many days before they were completely cleared
of the disease.

We were operating in an area that produced wheat and
raw cotton, and these became materials for the Japanese
army operations. At harvest time, we picked out areas for
surrounding, tortured the villagers, then plundered everything.

The mountains in the southern part of the province
had coal mines, and we plundered the coal by capturing
Chinese and forcing them to work in the mines. And
when we were not involved in major operations, we

would go out into our own immediate area on continuous three-day operations to see if there were any of the enemy around. On such occasions, we stole, tortured, and slaughtered people. The Chinese had a saying about us, that Japan had a "three–way complete policy: burned completely, killed completely, and pillaged completely." Yet, when we were doing those things, we had no sense of guilt or of doing anything wrong. It was for the emperor—for the country!

Select Bibliography

Asahi Shinbun. "Kitaman no kibyo wo seifuku." April 2, 1941.

Asahi Shinbun. "Kyu rikugun gun'i gakko atochi no jinkotsu kantei." April 23, 1992.

Asahi Shinbun. "Nomonhan jiken, chifusu kin nagashita." August 24, 1989.

Browne, Courtney. *Tojo: The Last Banzai.* New York: Paperback Library, Inc., 1967.

Cook, Haruko Taya and Cook, Theodore F. *Japan at War: an Oral History.* New York: The New Press, 1992.

Dallek, Robert. *Franklin D. Roosevelt and American Foreign Policy, 1932–1945.* New York: Oxford University Press, 1979.

———. "Development of Japanese Biological Warfare." Four articles based on investigation conducted by Lt. Col Thompson. USAFPAC Daily Intelligence Summary #1561, July 30, 1946; #1562, July 31, 1946; #1563, August 31, 1946; #1564, August 2, 1946. RG 4: USAFPAC. General Douglas MacArthur Memorial Archives and Library, Norfolk, Virginia.

Fish, Hamilton. *FDR: The Other Side of the Coin.* New York: Vantage Press, 1976.

Foreign Languages Publishing House. *Materials on the Trial of Former Servicemen of the Japanese Army Charged with Manufacturing and Employing Bacteriological Weapons.* Moscow: Foreign Languages Publishing House, 1950.

Han, Xiao. *731 butai no hanzai.* (Translated from Chinese into Japanese by Yamabe Yukiko) Tokyo: 31 Shobo, 1993.

Harris, Sheldon H. *Factories of Death*. London and New York: Routledge, 1994.

———. "Japanese Biological Warfare Research on Humans: A Case Study of Microbiology and Ethics." Presented at a conference entitled "The Microbiologist and Biological Defense Research: Ethics, Politics, and International Security," University of Maryland Baltimore County (UMBC) April 4–5, 1991. *Annals of the New York Academy of Sciences* 666 (1992): 21–52.

Hollinghorst, R.L. and Steer, Arthur. "Far East Command Conference on Epidemic Hemorrhagic Fever: Pathology of Epidemic Hemorrhagic Fever." *Annals of Internal Medicine* 38 (1953): 77–101.

Japan Times. "Toxic gas plant still uneasy topic." January 17, 1995.

Johnstone, Ralph. "Interview with Professor Tsuneishi Keiichi." *Tokyo Journal*. May 1994. 18–21.

———. "Japanese Violations of the Laws of War." Research Report #72 (Supplement No.2) 23 June 1945. RG 3: SWPA, ATIS. Item 7, "Other Violations: Bacterial Warfare." 9. General Douglas MacArthur Memorial Archives and Library, Norfolk, Virginia.

"Joho Tokushu." Broadcast on February 26, 1995 by TBS Network.

Pacific Stars and Stripes. "SCAP Locates and Questions General Ishii." February 27, 1946.

Kasahara, Shiro; Kitano, Masaji; et al. "Ryukosei shukketsu netsubyo no byogentai no kettei." *Nihon Byori Gakkaishi* 34 (1944): 3–5.

Mainichi Shinbun. "Senritsu no jintai jikken." November 27, 1981.

Maru Special. "I-go sensuikan." Tokyo: July 1977.

McNinch, Joseph H. "Far East Command Conference on Epidemic Hemorrhagic Fever: Introduction." *Annals of Internal Medicine* 38 (1953): 53–60.

Message, CINCFE to WDCSA. Nr. C-69946, February 7, 1947. "WC" 140. General Douglas MacArthur Memorial Archives and Library, Norfolk, Virginia.

Message, Washington (The Joint Chiefs of Staff) to CINCFE (MacArthur) Nr. W-94446, March 21, 1947. "WC" 141. General Douglas MacArthur Memorial Archives and Library, Norfolk, Virginia.

Message, CINCFE to WDCSA, Nr. C-51310, March 27, 1947. "WC" 142. General Douglas MacArthur Memorial Archives and Library, Norfolk, Virginia.

Message, Washington (WDGPO) to CINCFE, Nr. W-95265, April 2, 1947. "WC" 143. General Douglas MacArthur Memorial Archives and Library, Norfolk, Virginia.

Message, CINCFE to WDCID, TOO: 061015, May 6, 1947. "WC" 147. General Douglas MacArthur Memorial Archives and Library, Norfolk, Virginia.

Message, War (Chemical Corps) to CINCFE (G-2) (Chief Chemical Officer for Fell), Nr. W-98097, May 15, 1947. "WC" 149. General Douglas MacArthur Memorial Archives and Library, Norfolk, Virginia.

Message, War (WDSCA WO) to CINCFE (For Carpenter, Legal Sect. for Action), Nr. WAR 99277, June 3, 1947. "WC" 150. General Douglas MacArthur Memorial Archives and Library, Norfolk, Virginia.

Message, CINCFE (Carpenter, Legal Section, SCAP) to War (WDSCA WC), Nr. C-53169, June 6, 1947. "WC" 151. General Douglas MacArthur Memorial Archives and Library, Norfolk, Virginia.

Message, War (WDSCA WC) to CINCFE (Carpenter, Legal Sect.), Nr. War 80671, June 22, 1947. "WC" 154. General Douglas MacArthur Memorial Archives and Library, Norfolk, Virginia.

Message, CINCFE to War (WDSCA WC), Nr. C-53663, June 27, 1947. "WC" 155. General Douglas MacArthur Memorial Archives and Library, Norfolk, Virginia.

Message, JCOS to CINCFE (MacArthur), Nr. W-97605, March 14, 1948. "WC" 187. General Douglas MacArthur Memorial Archives and Library, Norfolk, Virginia.

Message, CSGID to CINCFE (G-2), Nr. WAR 87011, August 5, 1948. General Douglas MacArthur Memorial Archives and Library, Norfolk, Virginia.

Message, State Department Washington DC to SCAP (USPO-LAD) Tokyo, Nr. 251943 Z, December 26, 1949. General Douglas MacArthur Memorial Archives and Library, Norfolk, Virginia.

Message, State Department Washington DC to SCAP (USPO-LAD) Tokyo, Nr. 262208 Z, December 27, 1949. General Douglas MacArthur Memorial Archives and Library, Norfolk, Virginia.

Message, State Department Washington DC to SCAP (USPO-LAD) Tokyo, Nr. 011515 Z, January 2, 1950. General Douglas MacArthur Memorial Archives and Library, Norfolk, Virginia.

Message, State Department Washington DC to SCAP (USPO-LAD) Tokyo, Nr. 020845 Z, February 2, 1950. General Douglas MacArthur Memorial Archives and Library, Norfolk, Virginia.

Mori Masataka (producer) *Shinryaku (Part 5)*. Joei zenkoku renrakukai. Shizuoka, 1992.

———*Nihon wa Chugoku ni nani wo shita no.* Shizuoka: Joei zenkoku renrakukai, 1993. Supplement to documentary video series.

National Archives, Washington D.C. Department of Navy Records. Record Group 80. "Naval Aspects of Biological Warfare." Box 55.

National Archives, Washington D.C. Record Group 165. "Request of Russian Prosecutor for Permission to Interrogate Certain Japanese." File: SWNCC 351. Entry 468, Box 628.

National Archives, Washington D.C. Record Group 319. "Biological Warfare Activities and Capabilities of Foreign Nations." March 30, 1946. Box 101, Case 67/3.

National Archives, Suitland, Md. Record Group 84. State Department Washington DC to SCAP (USPOLAD) Tokyo Japan. Nr. 020845 Z. February 2, 1950. Folder 321.6 War Crimes 1950, Box 64, Location 4/64/12/2.

National Archives, Suitland, Md. Record Group 84. Letter. Ohta, Ichiro, Vice Minister for Foreign Affairs, The Gaimusho, Tokyo, to W.J. Sebald, Diplomatic Section, SCAP.

February 3, 1950. Folder 321.6 War Crimes 1950, Box 64, Location 4/64/12/2. Folder 321.6 War Crimes 1950, Box 64, Location 4/64/12/2.

National Archives, Suitland, Md. Record Group 84. Memorandum of Conversation. Office of the United States Political Advisor for Japan. Subject: Soviet Proposal for Trial of Emperor Hirohito. February 3, 1950. Folder 321.6 War Crimes 1950, Box 64, Location 4/64/12/2.

National Archives, Suitland, Md. Record Group 84. DA (SAOUS OUSFE) Washington DC to SCAP (Diplomatic) (Sebald) Tokyo. Nr W 99564, February 15, 1950. Folder 321.6 War Crimes 1950, Box 64, Location 4/64/12/2.

National Archives, Suitland, Md. Record Group 84. SCAP Tokyo to Dept of Army (SSOUS OUSFE) Washington DC. No. 259. March 15, 1950. Folder 321.6 War Crimes 1950, Box 64, Location 4/64/12/2.

National Archives, Suitland, Md. Record Group 84. State Dept Washington DC to CINCFE (US POLAD) Tokyo, Nr. 090252 Z. June 9, 1950. Folder 321.6 War Crimes 1950, Box 64, Location 4/64/12/2.

Nakagawa, Yonezo. Interview with author. Kyoto, Japan, April 1995.

"Odoroki momo no ki nijuseiki." Broadcast on November 25, 1944 by Asahi Television Network.

Okinawa Times. "Okinawa demo saikinsen sotei." January 25, 1994.

Okinawa Times. "Ito Kageaki." January 28, 1994.

Ota, Masakatsu. "731 Butai to senpan menseki." *Senso Sekinin Kenkyu.* Spring 1995. 90–95.

Phan, Ming Yen. "WW II germ lab secret." Singapore *Straits Times.* September 19, 1991.

———. "US Army records mention wartime germ lab in S'pore." Singapore *Straits Times.* September 25, 1991.

———. "Germ lab's head says work solely for research, vaccines." Singapore *Straits Times.* November 11, 1991.

Reischauer, Edwin O. *Japan: The Story of a Nation.* Tokyo: Charles E. Tuttle Co., 1970.

Renmin Ribao (domestic edition only). "You piao feng buo lian xian." December 24, 1994.

Sakura, Hajime. Telephone interview from Sapporo, Hokkaido with author. July 1995.

Sankei Shinbun. "Saikinsen—kaigun mo keikaku." August 8, 1977.

Seaman, Louis Livingston. *The Real Triumph of Japan: the Conquest of the Silent Foe.* New York: D. Appleton and Co., 1907.

Secretariat of the Unit 731 Exhibition. *731 Butai ten.* Magazine-style, 169-page catalog of exhibits and bibliographic material published by the umbrella group that organized the Unit 731 Exhibition.

South Manchuria Railway Co. 1933. Mukden. Pamphlet.

Terry, T. Phillip. *Terry's Guide to the Japanese Empire.* Boston & New York: Houghton Mifflin Co., 1933.

Tsuneishi, Keiichi. Igakushatachi no Soshiki Hanzai. Tokyo: Asahi Shinbunsha, 1994.

———. "The Research Guarded by Military Secrecy." *Historia Scientiarum* 30 (1986): 79–92.

———. Telephone interviews from Tokyo with author. June and July 1995.

"Unit 731—Did The Emperor Know?" Broadcast by British Independent Television on August 13, 1985.

van Courtland Moon, John Ellis. Biological Warfare Allegations: The Korean Case. Presented at a conference entitled "The Microbiologist and Biological Defense Research: Ethics, Politics, and International Security," University of Maryland Baltimore County (UMBC) April 4–5, 1991. *Annals of the New York Academy of Sciences,* 666 (1992): 53–83.

Warner, Dennis and Warner, Peggy, with Commander Seno, Sadao, JMSDF (Ret.). *The Sacred Warriors: Japan's Suicide Legions.* New York: Van Nostrand Reinhold Company, 1982.

Yamaguchi, Keiichiro. Interviews with author. Osaka and Kyoto, 1994 and 1995.

Yoshimura, Hisato. *Kiju Kaiso.* Kyoto: Kyoto Prefectural University of Medicine, Department of Physiology, 1984.